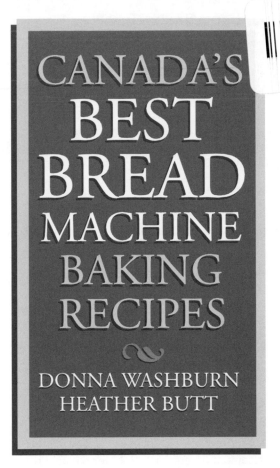

CANADA'S BEST BREAD MACHINE BAKING RECIPES

DONNA WASHBURN
HEATHER BUTT

Robert
ROSE

CANADA'S BEST BREAD MACHINE BAKING RECIPES

For complete cataloguing data, see page 4.

DESIGN, EDITORIAL & PRODUCTION:	MATTHEWS COMMUNICATIONS DESIGN INC.
PHOTOGRAPHY:	MARK T. SHAPIRO
ART DIRECTION/FOOD PHOTOGRAPHY:	SHARON MATTHEWS
FOOD STYLIST:	KATE BUSH
PROP STYLIST:	CHARLENE ERRICSON
MANAGING EDITOR:	PETER MATTHEWS
PROJECT EDITOR:	YVONNE TREMBLAY
INDEXER:	BARBARA SCHON
COLOR SCANS & FILM:	POINTONE GRAPHICS

We acknowledge the financial support of the Government of Canada through the Book Publishing Industry Development Program (BPIDP) for our publishing activities.

Canada

Published by: Robert Rose Inc. • 156 Duncan Mill Road, Suite 12
Toronto, Ontario, Canada M3B 2N2   Tel: (416) 449-3535

Printed in Canada

7 BP 02 01

CONTENTS

Canadian Cataloguing in Publication Data

Washburn, Donna

    Canada's best bread machine baking recipes

Includes index.

ISBN 0-7788-0003-2

1. Bread.   2. Automatic bread machines.   I. Butt, Heather.   II. Title.

TX769.W373 1999   641.8'15   C99-930019-9

Photo Prop Credits

The publisher and authors wish to express their appreciation to the following supplier of props used in the food photography appearing in this book:

Dishes, cutlery, glassware, linens and accessories: **TABLE OF CONTENTS**
Queeen's Quay Terminal, Toronto
(416) 203-1182

ACKNOWLEDGEMENTS

The aroma from the test kitchen permeates the neighborhood. Chocolate, cinnamon, apple, cheese and herbs furnish the appetizing fragrances of these tasty loaves.

Our test kitchen counters have been lined with over 30 bread machines — kneading, mixing, beeping and baking from early morning until late at night — testing and re-testing until the loaves were perfect. Each loaf was baked, weighed and sliced in several places — and, yes, tasted. Thank you to Philips Electronics, Proctor-Silex, Regal, Sunbeam/Oster, Toastmaster, West Bend, Black & Decker and Zojirushi for supplying the machines used in testing.

A special thanks to Molly Pocklington-Thompson, Nadya Antoniades and Jim Kopp of fermipan® and Lallemand Inc., and Monique Croteau of Five Roses for supplying yeast and flour for the recipe testing. Also to Brian Creighton of Myer's Bulk Foods, who filled orders just in the nick of time for speedy pick-up on rushed trips to Kingston.

A very special thank you to the team who took such care in making the bread look as good as it tastes, during the photography sessions. To Mark Shapiro of Mark Shapiro Photography, food stylist Kate Bush, art director Sharon Matthews, and prop stylist Charlene Erricson, thank you for the TLC the breads received.

Our thanks to our publisher, Bob Dees, and to Yvonne Tremblay, project editor for Robert Rose Inc., who knew Bob wanted to publish a bread machine cookbook and investigated our company. Also to Peter Matthews and the staff of Matthews Communications Design Inc. for working through all the exceptions involved in this cookbook's editorial, design, layout and production.

Last but by no means least, we want to thank those who have always been there — our husbands, for their support, words of wisdom and (of course) unbiased taste testing. A special thank you to our sons and the rest of our families for assistance supplied by each with their unique expertise.

Just ask us — are we tired of baking bread? The fragrance of baked bread is still warming to our hearts. We hope you have as many enjoyable hours baking the recipes from our cookbook as we have had developing them for you.

DEDICATION

We want to dedicate this book to our mothers, both of whom were career women — caring teachers by profession. By example, they instilled in us the important values of honesty, integrity and a strong desire to challenge ourselves to continue to grow in our lifelong search for knowledge. Without them, our friendship would never have developed and this book would never have been written.

Canada's Best Bread Machine Baking Recipes has been written for you, the person who cherishes homemade bread but can't remember life before your bread machine. We too can't get along without ours. First and most important, writing this cookbook has allowed two very good friends the opportunity to work together, in a business, doing work we love. We both enjoy the creativity of baking, the challenge of recipe development and of course we love to eat.

Both Professional Home Economists, we have university degrees in our field of study. Donna started Quality Professional Services in 1992 to develop recipes for small electrical appliances. Black & Decker was QPS's first customer. Recipes for the US and Canadian markets were developed for Black & Decker's bread machines. Heather became a partner in 1994. Today QPS publishes *The Bread Basket*, an international newsletter for bread machine owners. Besides developing recipes for fermipan® yeast, Lallemand Inc., we have become their test kitchen experts and manage their toll-free phone service. Philips Electronics use QPS to answer questions requiring a home economist for their toll-free phone service. We continue to develop recipes for a wide range of bread machine manufacturers.

Our training and professional values are tested daily as we attempt to satisfy and protect our customers and you, our readers. On one hand, we have the manufacturers for whom we do recipe development; on the other, we have you, the consumer, for whom we try to do our best by sharing our knowledge and expertise. Practicality is the keynote of our work.

We can assure you that all the recipes in this cookbook have been tested and re-tested to meet the highest standards of quality and appeal. Well over 1,000 pounds of flour, 36 tins of yeast, gallons of honey, pounds of cracked wheat, etc. etc. went into testing these recipes. Each and every dough was measured, cut, re-measured; every rising, timed and re-timed. The oven temperatures were checked, the baked dough tapped on the bottom, sides and top. We want to provide you the best possible recipes to guarantee your success and enjoyment using your bread machine.

Donna Washburn
Heather Butt

As you begin to use our cookbook and to choose recipes, remember to read our helpful hints and useful practical tips found in each chapter. Now, all that remains for you is just to bake bread, taste it with enthusiasm, and enjoy your handiwork. Happy bread baking everyone!

RECIPE SELECTION

The selection of recipes includes a mix ranging from old family favorites, often referred to as comfort foods, to some of the newest trends. Whether new or old, all have been modified for the bread machine. Some are just the old standbys but with a new twist.

Every recipe provides both the imperial and metric volume measures. It doesn't matter which you use, just choose one and be consistent. It is never recommended to mix and match types of measuring equipment. The recipes are not conversions but developed for the type of measuring you feel comfortable using. **It is most important that you measure accurately.**

Approximately half the recipes begin with the dough cycle, followed by forming, rising and baking. We have provided as much choice as possible with these. We don't like to make a recipe into one particular shape and don't feel that you need to either. Make your choices and enjoy the chance for lots of variety. Let your creativity shine through, and very soon you will feel comfortable enough to experiment and create shapes of your own. There is no better stress reliever than rolling up your sleeves, getting elbow deep in flour and working with a shaped dough.

ADJUSTING THE RECIPES

About the whole question of checking and adjusting the doughball — we thought we'd like to give you our philosophy about this subject. We develop recipes so that the guesswork is taken out of baking bread with your bread machine. We do not believe there is a need for you to guess whether the dough is too stiff or too sticky. Sweet and rye breads have stickier dough balls than basic whites just as oatmeal and pumpernickel loaves are denser than basic white. A friend of ours once complained that all breads from her bread machine were too much alike. You won't say that if you follow our recipes! Remember, all you really need to do is measure accurately, press the button and return when signalled. Relax! Leave the recipe development to us!

LOAF SIZE

The recipes for loaves in this cookbook were developed in two sizes — 1.5 pound and 2 pound. Today there are many extra-large horizontal and vertical 2-pound bread machine models on the market. We have marked an "L" (for "Large") beside loaves that will bake to the top of these baking pans. We strongly recommend you consult the chart below and follow the directions to determine which size of recipe will bake the best loaf in your particular model of bread machine. If your baking pan capacity is less than 12 cups (3 L), bake the smaller recipe size.

BREAD MACHINE BAKING PAN SIZE

Determine the volume of your baking pan by filling it with water, using a measuring cup. Consult the chart below to verify the size of recipe to use.

Machine Capacity and Loaf Size		
Loaf		Capacity of Baking Pan
Size	Weight	
Medium	1.5 lbs	6 to 9 cups (1.5 to 2.25 L)
Large	2 lbs	9 to 12 cups (2.25 to 3 L)
Extra Large	2.5 lbs	12 to 15 cups (3 to 4 L)

Hints For Successful Bread Machine Baking

1. Measure all the ingredients accurately.

2. Remove the baking pan from the bread machine when measuring and adding recipe ingredients; do not measure over the bread pan.

3. Follow your bread machine manufacturer's recommended order of adding recipe ingredients.

4. Consult your operating manual for the best ingredient temperature.

5. Keep dried fruits, grains and cereals away from the liquid in the pan.

6. Use the type of yeast specified in the recipe.

7. Make a well in the top of the flour for the yeast. It should not touch the liquid.

8. Keep cinnamon and garlic away from the yeast as they inhibit the rising.

9. Measure the fruit and nuts for the "add ingredients" signal and place them beside the bread machine before starting the machine.

10. Do not use the timer for recipes containing eggs, fresh milk, cheese and other perishables.

THE BREAD MACHINE PANTRY

Great baking requires the right ingredients. Here's a guide to the most important ingredients you'll be using for the recipes in this book. Additional detail can be found in the Glossary (page 184).

FLOUR

Flour makes up the largest part of any yeast bread. It provides the gluten, a protein, that forms the cell wall structure, trapping the gas bubbles and holding air, allowing the dough to rise. Only wheat and rye flours contain gluten.

Both all-purpose and bread flour can be used in Canada as both contain enough gluten (protein) to bake excellent loaves

Do not use cake-and-pastry or self-rising blends to bake breads in your bread machine.

Whether unbleached or bleached, all-purpose or bread flour will give the same baking results.

The bran in whole wheat flour supplies the fiber found in whole wheat products. The small amount of fat found in the germ makes long term storage in the freezer necessary. This prevents that fat from becoming rancid.

Most of the vitamins and minerals are found in the bran and germ.

Enrichment is a process that involves adding back the vitamins and minerals removed during the refining process of the flour.

Rye flour must always be used in combination with wheat flour in bread machine baking. Only small amounts can be used. Be careful when working with rye flour, because the gluten in it is not very elastic and becomes sticky with too much kneading. It can be purchased in light, medium and dark varieties. Only the intensity of color of the finished product will vary. We do not recommend that the amounts of rye flour be increased in any of the recipes.

To preserve its strength and ability to rise, store all flour to be used within a six-month period in an airtight container, in a cool, dry place. Do not store flour in the refrigerator as it picks up moisture. Freeze for long-term storage. Allow the flour to return to room temperature before using.

LIQUIDS

The liquids you use in these recipes can include water, milk, and fruit and vegetable juices.

Water tends to yield a crisper crust, while milk supplies some fat to bake a softer, more tender-textured loaf.

Both fluid milk and powdered milk in combination with water can be used in bread machines. Use the fluid milk of a fat content you prefer; homogenized, 2%, 1%, low-fat or skim. Skim milk powder and/or buttermilk powder should be used when setting the timer function. Consult the manufacturers' manual for the temperature of the milk to add to your bread machine. We find that unless there are a lot of cold ingredients in the recipe, cold milk from the refrigerator can be used.

Fruit juice will help intensify flavor and color. Purchase unsweetened fruit juices for consistent results. The amount of sugar and salt varies in juices. Read the label to be sure the product you purchase is a fruit juice and not a fruit drink. We recommend using the amount of each juice stated in the recipe.

SALT

Although the amount that is used in each recipe is small, it can **not** be omitted. Salt is very important as it controls the yeast's activity and prevents over-rising and thus collapsing of the loaf. Breads made without salt are very bland.

YEAST

Yeast eats the carbohydrates in flour and the sugar in the recipe to produce carbon dioxide gas that is trapped in the structure and causes dough to rise. The recipes in this cookbook were developed using bread machine yeast. We always recommend using the type of yeast called for in the recipe. Both bread machine and instant yeast are very active strains of yeast that can be added directly to the bread machine and don't require pre-activating.

Store a 2- to 3-month supply in the refrigerator in an airtight container. "Use before the expiry date" means to open before that date and use within a 2-month period. For long-term storage, yeast should be kept in an airtight container in the freezer. Do not transfer from one container to another as introducing extra air can shorten the life of yeast.

Perform this test for freshness if you suspect that the yeast has become less active. Dissolve 1 tsp (5 mL) sugar in 1/2 cup (125 mL) luke-warm (tepid) water. Add 2 tsp (10 mL) yeast and stir gently. In 10 minutes, mixture should have a strong yeasty smell and be foamy. If not, the yeast is too old — time to buy fresh yeast!

SUGARS

Sugar provides food for the yeast and flavor to the dough. Granulated sugar, packed brown sugar, honey and molasses can be used interchangeably. Results will vary slightly in color, flavor and texture.

Aspartame-based sugar substitutes can be used, but not saccharin-based. Substitute equal amounts for the sugar in the recipe.

FATS

Fat gives the crust its tenderness and the loaf its softness. It also helps to delay bread from getting stale by retaining moisture. The type of fat used becomes a matter of preference. The loaves will vary slightly. Shortening, margarine, butter or oil can be interchanged. Do not use diet, low-calorie margarine as it has a higher water content. The size and texture of the loaf will be affected.

Cheese and the yolk of an egg contributes to the fat in some recipes. Use large size eggs directly from the refrigerator. Do not use recipes containing eggs or cheese with the timer. When measuring cheese, do not pack. If desired, small cubes of cheese can replace shredded, since it melts during baking.

SEEDS, NUTS AND GRAINS

These are added to supply flavor and body to the breads while adding fiber, vitamins and minerals. This category includes cereals such as Red River, 7-grain, 12-grain, cracked wheat, bulgur and cornmeal, in addition to seeds, nuts and dried fruits.

To prevent the dried fruit from breaking up or puréeing, add at the "add ingredient" signal or at least 5 minutes before the end of the last knead.

OTHER FLAVORING AGENTS

Herbs and spices, dried fruits, garlic, onions and chocolate add to the flavor of the recipes. This group includes two enemies of yeast — cinnamon and garlic. Care must be taken to keep these ingredients from touching the yeast. Do not add extra amounts of either cinnamon or garlic. Resulting loaves will be short, heavy and very dense.

BEYOND THE BASICS

Here you will find breads your whole family will enjoy. They're more flavorful than basic recipes typically featured in most bread machine manuals. Try the Chunky Chili Cornbread (with whole corn kernels) or the subtle sweetness of Roasted Garlic Bread.

Cheddar Beer Bread

1.5 LB (750 G)		
1 1/4 cups	beer	300 mL
1 1/4 tsp	salt	6 mL
2 tbsp	granulated sugar	25 mL
3 cups	all-purpose flour or bread flour	750 mL
1/3 cup	buttermilk powder	75 mL
1/2 cup	shredded old Cheddar cheese	125 mL
2 tbsp	grated Parmesan cheese	25 mL
1 1/4 tsp	bread machine yeast	6 mL

2 LB (1 KG)		
1 1/2 cups	beer	375 mL
1 1/2 tsp	salt	7 mL
2 tbsp	granulated sugar	25 mL
3 1/2 cups	all-purpose flour or bread flour	950 mL
1/2 cup	buttermilk powder	125 mL
3/4 cup	shredded old Cheddar cheese	175 mL
1/4 cup	grated Parmesan cheese	50 mL
1 1/2 tsp	bread machine yeast	7 mL

Is there a cheese lover who doesn't enjoy the combination of cheese and beer? What a perfect loaf!

TIP

Add 1/4 tsp (1 mL) dry mustard powder to sharpen the cheese flavor.

VARIATION

Replace beer with an equal amount of water or "lite" beer.

1. Measure ingredients into baking pan in the order recommended by the manufacturer. Insert pan into the oven chamber.
2. Select **Sweet Cycle**.

Chunky Chili Cornbread

1.5 LB (750 G)		
1 1/4 cups	water	300 mL
1	egg	1
1/4 cup	skim milk powder	50 mL
1 tsp	salt	5 mL
2 tbsp	granulated sugar	25 mL
2 tbsp	shortening	25 mL
3 cups	all-purpose flour or bread flour	750 mL
1/3 cup	cornmeal	75 mL
2/3 cup	thawed frozen corn kernels, well drained	150 mL
1 1/2 tsp	crushed red chili peppers	7 mL
1 tsp	bread machine yeast	5 mL

2 LB (1 KG)		L
1 1/3 cups	water	325 mL
1	egg	1
1/4 cup	skim milk powder	50 mL
1 tsp	salt	5 mL
2 tbsp	granulated sugar	25 mL
2 tbsp	shortening	25 mL
3 2/3 cups	all-purpose flour or bread flour	900 mL
2/3 cup	cornmeal	150 mL
3/4 cup	thawed frozen corn kernels, well drained	175 mL
2 tsp	crushed red chili peppers	10 mL
1 1/2 tsp	bread machine yeast	7 mL

1. Measure ingredients into baking pan in the order recommended by the manufacturer. Insert pan into the oven chamber.
2. Select **Basic Cycle**.

Summer brings juicy sweet ears of fresh corn to the farmer's market, but this loaf can be a year-round treasure.

TIP

Thaw the frozen corn kernels completely and drain well before adding.

The 2 lb (1 kg) recipe makes a large loaf. It can be baked in a 2.5 lb (1.25 kg) machine. If you have a small bread pan, prepare the 1.5 lb (750 g) recipe.

VARIATION

Replace frozen corn with leftover cooked corn sliced from the cob.

Green Peppercorn Mustard Rye

1.5 LB (750 G)		
1 1/4 cups	water	300 mL
1/4 cup	green peppercorn mustard or Dijon mustard	50 mL
1/4 cup	skim milk powder	50 mL
1/2 tsp	salt	2 mL
1 tbsp	packed brown sugar	15 mL
2 tbsp	olive oil	25 mL
3/4 cup	whole wheat flour	175 mL
2 cups	all-purpose flour or bread flour	500 mL
2/3 cup	rye flour	150 mL
2 tsp	dill seeds	10 mL
1 1/4 tsp	bread machine yeast	6 mL

2 LB (1 KG)		
1 1/3 cups	water	325 mL
1/3 cup	green peppercorn mustard or Dijon mustard	75 mL
1/4 cup	skim milk powder	50 mL
3/4 tsp	salt	3 mL
2 tbsp	packed brown sugar	25 mL
2 tbsp	olive oil	25 mL
1 cup	whole wheat flour	250 mL
2 cups	all-purpose flour or bread flour	500 mL
3/4 cup	rye flour	200 mL
1 tbsp	dill seeds	15 mL
1 3/4 tsp	bread machine yeast	8 mL

A different loaf every time! Try the variety of flavored mustards on the market; each is unique.

TIP

Do not substitute "Dijonnaise" for the Dijon mustard. It is a totally different product — and too high in fat.

VARIATION

Substitute an equal amount of tarragon mustard for the coarsely ground green peppercorn mustard.

1. Measure ingredients into baking pan in the order recommended by the manufacturer. Insert pan into the oven chamber.
2. Select **Whole Wheat Cycle**.

Honey Dijon with Bits of Bacon

1.5 LB (750 G)		
1 1/4 cups	water	300 mL
2 tbsp	honey Dijon mustard	25 mL
1/4 cup	skim milk powder	50 mL
1 tsp	salt	5 mL
2 tbsp	honey	25 mL
1 tbsp	shortening	15 mL
3 cups	all-purpose flour or bread flour	750 mL
3	slices crisp bacon	3
3/4 tsp	bread machine yeast	3 mL

2 LB (1 KG)		L
1 1/2 cups	water	375 mL
1/4 cup	honey Dijon mustard	50 mL
1/4 cup	skim milk powder	50 mL
1 1/4 tsp	salt	6 mL
2 tbsp	honey	25 mL
1 tbsp	shortening	15 mL
3 1/2 cups	all-purpose flour or bread flour	875 mL
4	slices crisp bacon	4
3/4 tsp	bread machine yeast	4 mL

1. Measure ingredients into baking pan in the order recommended by the manufacturer. Insert pan into the oven chamber.
2. Select **Sweet Cycle**.

A hint of sweet mustard contrasts with the savory, smoky bacon to give this loaf a unique flavor.

TIP

Cook the bacon in the microwave for a crisper texture. Drain it well on paper towels.

VARIATION

Prepared mustard may be substituted for Honey Dijon.

Jalapeno Cheese Bread

1.5 LB (750 G)		
1 1/4 cups	water	300 mL
1/2 tsp	hot pepper sauce	2 mL
1/4 cup	skim milk powder	50 mL
1 1/2 tsp	salt	7 mL
1 tbsp	granulated sugar	15 mL
3 1/4 cups	all-purpose flour or bread flour	800 mL
3/4 cup	cornmeal	175 mL
2 tsp	crushed dried jalapeno peppers	10 mL
1/2 cup	shredded old Cheddar cheese	125 mL
1 1/4 tsp	bread machine yeast	6 mL

2 LB (1 KG)		
1 1/3 cups	water	325 mL
1 tsp	hot pepper sauce	5 mL
1/4 cup	skim milk powder	50 mL
1 1/2 tsp	salt	7 mL
2 tbsp	granulated sugar	25 mL
3 1/2 cups	all-purpose flour or bread flour	875 mL
1 cup	cornmeal	250 mL
1 tbsp	crushed dried jalapeno peppers	15 mL
2/3 cup	shredded old Cheddar cheese	150 mL
1 1/2 tsp	bread machine yeast	7 mL

Adjust the quantity of hot pepper sauce and dried jalapenos to determine the "heat" of this delightful loaf.

TIP

Try using the last part of this loaf to make breadcrumbs. They're great as a spicy coating for baked chicken.

VARIATION

Fresh jalapeno peppers may be substituted for dried, but the loaf will be shorter and heavier.

For a slightly nutty and delicate tang, try Monterey Jack instead of Cheddar cheese.

1. Measure ingredients into baking pan in the order recommended by the manufacturer. Insert pan into the oven chamber.
2. Select **Sweet Cycle**.

Maritime Brown Bread

1.5 LB (750 G)		
1 1/4 cups	water	300 mL
1/4 cup	skim milk powder	50 mL
1 1/4 tsp	salt	5 mL
2 tbsp	packed brown sugar	25 mL
1 tbsp	molasses	15 mL
2 tbsp	shortening	25 mL
2 cups	whole wheat flour	500 mL
1 cup	all-purpose flour or bread flour	250 mL
1 tsp	bread machine yeast	5 mL

2 LB (1 KG)		
1 1/2 cups	water	380 mL
1/4 cup	skim milk powder	50 mL
1 1/2 tsp	salt	7 mL
1/4 cup	packed brown sugar	50 mL
2 tbsp	molasses	25 mL
2 tbsp	shortening	25 mL
2 1/2 cups	whole wheat flour	625 mL
1 1/2 cups	all-purpose flour or bread flour	375 mL
1 1/4 tsp	bread machine yeast	6 mL

What would Saturday night be on the east coast of North America without molasses-flavored baked beans and brown bread? Try our updated version for your bread machine.

TIP

Store molasses in the refrigerator. Microwave a few seconds before using for easier measuring.

VARIATION

Another regional treasure, maple syrup, can be substituted for the molasses to provide sweetness in either the beans or the brown bread. Or use a combination of both.

1. Measure ingredients into baking pan in the order recommended by the manufacturer. Insert pan into the oven chamber.
2. Select **Whole Wheat Cycle.**

New England Anadama Bread

1.5 LB (750 G)		
1 1/4 cups	water	300 mL
1/4 cup	skim milk powder	50 mL
1 tsp	salt	5 mL
3 tbsp	molasses	40 mL
2 tbsp	shortening	25 mL
3 cups	all-purpose flour or bread flour	750 mL
1/3 cup	cornmeal	75 mL
1 1/4 tsp	bread machine yeast	6 mL

2 LB (1 KG)		
1 1/2 cups	water	375 mL
1/4 cup	skim milk powder	50 mL
1 1/2 tsp	salt	7 mL
1/4 cup	molasses	50 mL
2 tbsp	shortening	25 mL
3 1/2 cups	all-purpose flour or bread flour	875 mL
1/2 cup	cornmeal	125 mL
1 1/2 tsp	bread machine yeast	7 mL

Named for Anna, a farmer's wife who refused to bake for her husband and who ran off with a tradesman. Upon discovering this, it is rumored the farmer was heard whispering "Anna damn her" as he kneaded cornmeal mush, starter, molasses and flour for his dinner.

TIP

Before measuring the molasses, dip the measuring spoon into hot water.

VARIATION

This loaf has a strong molasses flavor. For a milder flavor, substitute 1 tbsp (15 mL) brown sugar for 1 tbsp (15 mL) of the molasses.

1. Measure ingredients into baking pan in the order recommended by the manufacturer. Insert pan into the oven chamber.

2. Select **Basic Cycle**.

Oatmeal Raisin Bread

1.5 LB (750 G)		
1 1/4 cups	water	300 mL
1 1/4 tsp	salt	6 mL
2 tbsp	granulated sugar	25 mL
2 tbsp	shortening	25 mL
3 cups	all-purpose flour or bread flour	750 mL
1/3 cup	oatmeal	75 mL
1/2 cup	buttermilk powder	125 mL
1 1/4 tsp	bread machine yeast	6 mL
1 cup	raisins	250 mL

2 LB (1 KG)		
1 1/3 cups	water	325 mL
1 1/2 tsp	salt	7 mL
3 tbsp	granulated sugar	40 mL
3 tbsp	shortening	40 mL
3 cups	all-purpose flour or bread flour	750 mL
1/2 cup	oatmeal	125 mL
1/2 cup	buttermilk powder	125 mL
1 1/2 tsp	bread machine yeast	7 mL
1 1/3 cups	raisins	325 mL

1. Measure all ingredients *except raisins* into baking pan in the order recommended by the manufacturer. Insert pan into the oven chamber.
2. Select **Basic Cycle** or **Sweet Cycle**.
3. Add raisins at the "add ingredient" signal.

Oats make this loaf high in fiber — higher than an ordinary sweet raisin bread.

TIP

Add oat bran or cooked whole oat kernels for an "oatier" flavor.

VARIATION

Increase the fiber by adding 2 tbsp (25 mL) oat bran. The top may vary slightly, but the loaf will be delicious.

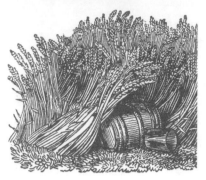

Old-Fashioned Goodness Cracked Wheat Bread

1.5 LB (750 G)		
1 1/3 cups	water	325 mL
1/4 cup	skim milk powder	50 mL
1 1/4 tsp	salt	5 mL
1 tbsp	honey	15 mL
2 tbsp	shortening	25 mL
2 3/4 cups	whole wheat flour	700 mL
1/2 cup	cracked wheat	125 mL
3/4 tsp	bread machine yeast	4 mL

2 LB (1 KG)		
1 1/2 cups	water	375 mL
1/4 cup	skim milk powder	50 mL
1 1/2 tsp	salt	7 mL
2 tbsp	honey	25 mL
2 tbsp	shortening	25 mL
3 cups	whole wheat flour	750 mL
3/4 cup	cracked wheat	175 mL
1 1/4 tsp	bread machine yeast	5 mL

Here's an old favorite, updated and adapted for your bread machine.

TIP

Substitute 3 1/4 cups (800 mL) wheat blend flour for the whole wheat flour and cracked wheat in the smaller loaf and 3 3/4 cups (925 mL) in the larger loaf.

Select Basic Cycle.

Keep cracked wheat from coming into contact with the water when you bake this loaf. Cracked wheat quickly absorbs water resulting in a shorter and heavier loaf.

VARIATION

Substituting an equal amount of bulgur for the cracked wheat results in a nuttier flavor and rougher texture.

1. Measure ingredients into baking pan in the order recommended by the manufacturer. Insert pan into the oven chamber.
2. Select **Whole Wheat Cycle**.

Raisin Malt Bread

1.5 LB (750 G)		
1 1/4 cups	water	300 mL
1/4 cup	skim milk powder	50 mL
1 1/2 tsp	salt	7 mL
2 tbsp	molasses	25 mL
2 tbsp	shortening	25 mL
2 cups	whole wheat flour	500 mL
1 1/4 cups	all-purpose flour or bread flour	300 mL
1/4 cup	malt powder	50 mL
1 1/2 tsp	bread machine yeast	7 mL
1/2 cup	raisins	125 mL

2 LB (1 KG)		
1 1/2 cups	water	375 mL
1/4 cup	skim milk powder	50 mL
1 1/2 tsp	salt	7 mL
2 tbsp	molasses	25 mL
2 tbsp	shortening	25 mL
2 2/3 cups	whole wheat flour	650 mL
1 1/2 cups	all-purpose flour or bread flour	375 mL
1/3 cup	malt powder	75 mL
1 1/2 tsp	bread machine yeast	7 mL
2/3 cup	raisins	150 mL

A traditional English favorite, this rich, dark-brown loaf is lightly sweetened with malt powder.

TIP

The added malt will keep the loaf fresh longer.

Store malt powder in an airtight container; it lumps with a small amount of moisture. Sift before adding, if necessary.

VARIATION

Prepare using the Dough Cycle, then bake in coffee tins for loaves with the traditional ridged edges.

1. Measure all ingredients *except the raisins* into baking pan in the order recommended by the manufacturer. Insert pan into the oven chamber.
2. Select **Basic** or **Whole Wheat Cycle**.
3. Add raisins at the "add ingredient" signal.

Roasted Garlic Bread

Cloves of fresh garlic, roasted in the oven, give a sweet, mild garlic aroma and flavor to this loaf.

TIP

Use 2 drops of olive oil for each bulb when roasting garlic. Extra oil will cause the loaf to be short and dense. (See Glossary, page 184)

Avoid the temptation to add more garlic, as it inhibits the yeast. Too much garlic and the loaf will be short and heavy.

VARIATION

For a stronger, more-prominent garlic flavor, serve toasted or warmed with either garlic butter or a garlic-flavored spread.

1.5 LB (750 G)		
1 1/4 cups	water	300 mL
1/4 cup	skim milk powder	50 mL
1 tsp	salt	5 mL
2 tbsp	honey	25 mL
2 tbsp	olive oil	25 mL
4	cloves roasted garlic	4
3 1/4 cups	all-purpose flour or bread flour	800 mL
3/4 tsp	bread machine yeast	4 mL

2 LB (1 KG)		
1 1/2 cups	water	375 mL
1/4 cup	skim milk powder	50 mL
1 1/2 tsp	salt	8 mL
3 tbsp	honey	45 mL
2 tbsp	olive oil	25 mL
6	cloves roasted garlic	6
3 3/4 cups	all-purpose flour or bread flour	950 mL
3/4 tsp	bread machine yeast	4 mL

1. Measure ingredients into baking pan in the order recommended by the manufacturer. Insert pan into the oven chamber.
2. Select **Sweet Cycle**.

Rosemary Caesar Bread

1.5 LB (750 G)		
1 1/4 cups	tomato vegetable juice	300 mL
1 tbsp	granulated sugar	15 mL
1 tbsp	olive oil	15 mL
3 1/4 cups	all-purpose flour or bread flour	800 mL
1/3 cup	snipped sun-dried tomatoes	75 mL
1/4 cup	snipped fresh rosemary	50 mL
1/4 tsp	paprika	1 mL
1 1/4 tsp	bread machine yeast	6 mL

2 LB (1 KG)		
1 1/2 cups	tomato vegetable juice	375 mL
2 tbsp	granulated sugar	25 mL
2 tbsp	shortening	25 mL
3 1/2 cups	all-purpose flour or bread flour	875 mL
1/2 cup	snipped sun-dried tomatoes	125 mL
1/3 cup	snipped fresh rosemary	75 mL
1/2 tsp	paprika	3 mL
1 1/2 tsp	bread machine yeast	8 mL

1. Measure ingredients into baking pan in the order recommended by the manufacturer. Insert pan into the oven chamber.
2. Select **Basic Cycle**.

The robust flavor of fresh rosemary combined with the deep red of the tomato-vegetable juice will bring compliments every time.

TIP

Large amounts of liquids, such as vegetable tomato juice, should be warmed to room temperature for higher, more open-textured loaves .

Use dry, not oil-packed, sun-dried tomatoes.

To soften sun-dried tomatoes, pour boiling water over them and let them soak for 10 minutes. Drain well and pat dry with a paper towel.

VARIATION

Substitute 1 to 2 tbsp (15 to 25 mL) garlic powder for the fresh rosemary. An equal amount of tomato juice can be substituted for the tomato vegetable juice.

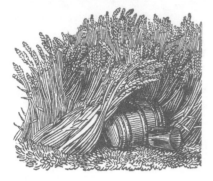

Sally Lunn Bread

1.5 LB (750 G)		
1 cup	milk	250 mL
1	egg	1
3/4 tsp	salt	3 mL
3 tbsp	granulated sugar	45 mL
2 tbsp	butter	25 mL
3 1/4 cups	all-purpose flour or bread flour	800 mL
1 tsp	bread machine yeast	5 mL

2 LB (1 KG)		L
1 1/4 cups	milk	300 mL
1	egg	1
1 1/4 tsp	salt	6 mL
1/4 cup	granulated sugar	50 mL
3 tbsp	butter	45 mL
3 1/2 cups	all-purpose flour or bread flour	875 mL
3/4 tsp	bread machine yeast	4 mL

1. Measure ingredients into baking pan in the order recommended by the manufacturer. Insert pan into the oven chamber.
2. Select **Sweet Cycle**.

Here's an updated version of Grandma's favorite. This rich, butter-and-egg bread traditionally is made in a ring mold and served hot from the oven.

TIP

Use large eggs straight from the refrigerator for bread machine recipes. Warm the milk to room temperature before adding.

Recipes containing eggs, milk and butter should not be baked using the timer.

VARIATION

Substitute 1/3 cup (75 mL) buttermilk powder and 1 cup (250 mL) water for every cup of milk required in the recipe.

Sour Cherry Almond Loaf

1.5 LB (750 G)		
1 1/4 cups	milk	300 mL
1/4 tsp	almond extract	1 mL
1	egg	1
1 1/2 tsp	salt	7 mL
1 tbsp	honey	15 mL
1 tbsp	shortening	15 mL
3 1/2 cups	all-purpose flour or bread flour	875 mL
1 1/2 tsp	bread machine yeast	7 mL
1/2 cup	dried sour red cherries	125 mL
1/2 cup	toasted slivered almonds	125 mL

2 LB (1 KG)		
1 1/3 cups	milk	325 mL
1/2 tsp	almond extract	2 mL
2	eggs	2
1 1/2 tsp	salt	7 mL
2 tbsp	honey	25 mL
2 tbsp	shortening	25 mL
3 3/4 cups	all-purpose flour or bread flour	950 mL
1 1/4 tsp	bread machine yeast	6 mL
2/3 cup	dried sour red cherries	150 mL
2/3 cup	toasted slivered almonds	150 mL

Nuggets of dried sour cherries and slivered almonds give this loaf a festive appearance.

TIP

Toast the almonds on a baking sheet in a 350° F (180° C) oven for 10 minutes. Remove when lightly browned. The almonds will continue to darken as they cool.

VARIATION

Other dried fruits — such as blueberries, cranberries, apples, raisins or apricots — may be used instead of cherries.

1. Measure all ingredients *except the sour cherries and toasted almonds* into baking pan in the order recommended by the manufacturer. Insert pan into the oven chamber.
2. Select **Sweet Cycle**.
3. Add the cherries and almonds at the "add ingredient" signal.

Tex-Mex Bread with Monterey Jack and Chilies

1.5 LB (750 G)		
1 cup	water	250 mL
1/4 cup	chopped canned green chilies	50 mL
1/2 tsp	salt	2 mL
1 tbsp	granulated sugar	15 mL
3 1/2 cups	all-purpose flour or bread flour	875 mL
1/2 cup	shredded Monterey Jack cheese	125 mL
4	slices crisp bacon, crumbled	4
3/4 tsp	bread machine yeast	4 mL

2 LB (1 KG)		
1 1/4 cups	water	300 mL
1/3 cup	chopped canned green chilies	75 mL
1 tsp	salt	5 mL
1 tbsp	granulated sugar	15 mL
3 3/4 cups	all-purpose flour or bread flour	950 mL
1/2 cup	shredded Monterey Jack cheese	125 mL
6	slices crisp bacon, crumbled	6
1 tsp	bread machine yeast	5 mL

1. Measure ingredients into baking pan in the order recommended by the manufacturer. Insert pan into the oven chamber.
2. Select **Sweet Cycle**.

The unique blend of savory, smoke and spices make this loaf a perfect accompaniment to home-made stew on a cold winter's night.

TIP

Be sure to cook bacon until crisp, then drain on a paper towel.

Serve yogurt as an accompaniment to cool the palate.

VARIATION

To increase the heat of the loaf, add hot pepper sauce or crushed red chili peppers.

LOW-FAT AND FLAVORFUL

Canada's "Guidelines for Healthy Eating" recommends we choose lower-fat foods more often. Bake these delicious breads containing little or no added fat.

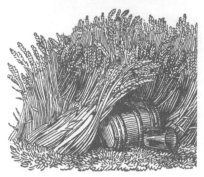

Apple Cinnamon Sticky Buns

MAKES 18 BUNS		

Two 8-inch (2 L) square pans, lightly greased
Preheat oven to 350° F (180° C)

1/2 cup	unsweetened applesauce	125 mL
1/2 cup	grated apple	125 mL
2	egg whites	2
1/2 tsp	salt	2 mL
3 tbsp	granulated sugar	45 mL
1 tbsp	shortening	15 mL
1 cup	whole wheat flour	250 mL
2 cups	all-purpose flour or bread flour	500 mL
2 tsp	bread machine yeast	10 mL

APPLE CINNAMON FILLING		
3 cups	coarsely chopped apples	750 mL
1 cup	raisins	250 mL
1/4 cup	honey	50 mL
2 tsp	cinnamon	10 mL
1 tsp	nutmeg	5 mL

Enjoy the old-fashioned flavors of apple and cinnamon in these low-fat sticky buns.

TIP

Choose Granny Smith or another quality baking apple for the filling.

VARIATION

Try this Cranberry-Orange Filling: Mix together 2 cups (500 mL) whole cranberry sauce and 1 tbsp (15 mL) orange zest.

Substitute raspberries for half the apples in the filling.

1. Measure ingredients into baking pan in the order recommended by the manufacturer. Insert pan into the oven chamber. Select **Dough Cycle**.
2. Meanwhile, prepare the filling: Gently combine the filling ingredients; set aside.
3. Remove prepared dough to a lightly floured board; cover with a large bowl and let rest for 10 to 15 minutes. Divide the dough in half. Roll out each into a 12- by 9-inch (30 by 23 cm) rectangle.
4. Spread half of the filling to within 1/2 inch (1 cm) of the edges. Pinch dough together. Beginning at a long side, roll up jellyroll style. Pinch to seal the seam. Cut into 9 equal slices. Place cut-side up in prepared pan. Repeat with remaining half of the dough.

5. Cover pans and let dough rise in a warm, draft-free place for 30 to 45 minutes or until doubled in volume.

6. Bake in preheated oven for 30 to 35 minutes or until the buns sound hollow when tapped on the bottom. If necessary, cover loosely with foil for the last 10 to 15 minutes to prevent over-browning. Invert the buns onto a serving plate; carefully remove the pan.

Flavor-enhancers for low-fat breads

Add any one of the following.
Do not exceed the amounts suggested.

1/4 cup	minced dried onion	50 mL
1/4 cup	snipped sun-dried tomatoes (not oil-packed)	50 mL
1/4 cup	snipped fresh herbs such as parsley, basil, chives	50 mL
2 tbsp	orange zest	25 mL
2 tbsp	unsweetened applesauce	25 mL
2 tbsp	mashed overripe banana	25 mL
2 tbsp	shredded carrot	25 mL
2 tsp	lemon zest	10 mL
2 tsp	freshly squeezed lemon juice	10 mL

Buttermilk Cracked Wheat Loaf

1.5 LB (750 G)		
1 1/4 cups	water	300 mL
1 1/4 tsp	salt	6 mL
2 tbsp	honey	25 mL
1 tbsp	shortening	15 mL
1 1/2 cups	whole wheat flour	375 mL
1 1/4 cups	all-purpose flour or bread flour	300 mL
3/4 cup	cracked wheat	175 mL
1/3 cup	buttermilk powder	75 mL
1 1/4 tsp	bread machine yeast	6 mL

2 LB (1 KG)		L
1 1/2 cups	water	375 mL
1 1/2 tsp	salt	7 mL
2 tbsp	honey	25 mL
2 tbsp	shortening	25 mL
1 1/2 cups	whole wheat flour	375 mL
2 cups	all-purpose flour or bread flour	500 mL
3/4 cup	cracked wheat	175 mL
1/2 cup	buttermilk powder	125 mL
1 1/2 tsp	bread machine yeast	7 mL

A bit of tang, a soft texture and a nutty crunch — all rolled into one.

TIP

Despite its name, buttermilk is actually low in fat. It also adds tenderness to the crumb of this bread.

VARIATION

Substitute 1 cup (250 mL) fresh buttermilk for 1/3 cup (75 mL) buttermilk powder and 1 cup (250 mL) water

1. Measure ingredients into baking pan in the order recommended by the manufacturer. Insert pan into the oven chamber.
2. Select **Whole Wheat Cycle**.

Buttermilk White Bread

1.5 LB (750 G)		
1 1/4 cups	water	325 mL
1 1/4 tsp	salt	6 mL
1 tbsp	granulated sugar	15 mL
1 tbsp	shortening	15 mL
3 1/2 cups	all-purpose flour or bread flour	875 mL
1/3 cup	buttermilk powder	75 mL
1 tsp	bread machine yeast	5 mL

2 LB (1 KG)		L
1 1/2 cups	water	375 mL
1 1/2 tsp	salt	7 mL
2 tbsp	granulated sugar	25 mL
2 tbsp	shortening	25 mL
3 3/4 cups	all-purpose flour or bread flour	925 mL
1/2 cup	buttermilk powder	125 mL
1 1/4 tsp	bread machine yeast	6 mL

1. Measure ingredients into baking pan in the order recommended by the manufacturer. Insert pan into the oven chamber.
2. Select **Basic Cycle**.

The texture and flavor of this loaf reminds us of days gone by when Grandma baked her recipe for white bread.

TIP

Add the buttermilk powder after the flour. It clumps when added with the liquids.

VARIATION

If buttermilk powder is unavailable, substitute 1/4 cup (50 mL) skim milk powder in either the 1.5 lb or 2 lb recipe.

Carrot Lovers' Poppy Seed Bread

1.5 LB (750 G)		
3/4 cup	water	175 mL
1/4 cup	skim milk powder	50 mL
1 1/4 tsp	salt	6 mL
3 tbsp	honey	45 mL
1 tbsp	vegetable oil	15 mL
2 cups	whole wheat flour	500 mL
1 cup	all-purpose flour or bread flour	250 mL
1 cup	grated carrots	250 mL
1/4 cup	poppy seeds	50 mL
2 tsp	orange zest	10 mL
1 tsp	dried thyme	5 mL
1 3/4 tsp	bread machine yeast	8 mL

2 LB (1 KG)		
1 cup	water	250 mL
1/4 cup	skim milk powder	50 mL
1 1/2 tsp	salt	7 mL
1/4 cup	honey	50 mL
2 tbsp	vegetable oil	25 mL
2 1/2 cups	whole wheat flour	650 mL
1 1/2 cups	all-purpose flour or bread flour	375 mL
1 1/4 cups	grated carrots	300 mL
1/3 cup	poppy seeds	75 mL
1 tbsp	orange zest	15 mL
1 1/4 tsp	dried thyme	6 mL
1 3/4 tsp	bread machine yeast	8 mL

Here's an exceptionally attractive loaf — confetti dots of bright orange carrot contrasting with the dark poppy seeds.

TIP

Any extra grated carrot can be frozen for later use.

To prevent the carrot from turning brown, make sure it doesn't touch the liquid.

VARIATION

Substitute unpeeled, grated, small zucchini for part or all of the carrots.

1. Measure ingredients into baking pan in the order recommended by the manufacturer. Insert pan into the oven chamber.
2. Use **Basic** or **Whole Wheat Cycle**.

CHUNKY CHILI CORNBREAD (PAGE 13) ➤

Cottage Cheese Dill Bread

1.5 LB (750 G)		
1 1/4 cups	water	300 mL
1/3 cup	low-fat cottage cheese	75 mL
1 1/4 tsp	salt	6 mL
1 tbsp	granulated sugar	15 mL
1 tbsp	shortening	15 mL
3 1/2 cups	all-purpose flour or bread flour	875 mL
1 tbsp	snipped fresh dill	15 mL
1 1/2 tsp	bread machine yeast	7 mL

2 LB (1 KG)		L
1 1/3 cups	water	325 mL
1/2 cup	low-fat cottage cheese	125 mL
1 1/2 tsp	salt	7 mL
2 tbsp	granulated sugar	25 mL
2 tbsp	shortening	25 mL
3 3/4 cups	all-purpose flour or bread flour	925 mL
2 tbsp	snipped fresh dill	25 mL
1 1/4 tsp	bread machine yeast	6 mL

1. Measure ingredients into baking pan in the order recommended by the manufacturer. Insert pan into the oven chamber.
2. Select **Basic Cycle**.

In this light loaf, cottage cheese (naturally low in fat) replaces some of the fat in a traditional white bread.

TIP

Choose a creamy or small-curd cottage cheese for smoother blending. Read the label to select and identify the fat content of the cottage cheese you prefer.

VARIATION

Substitute dill seeds for the fresh dill.

◄ CARROT LOVERS' POPPY SEED BREAD (PAGE 32)

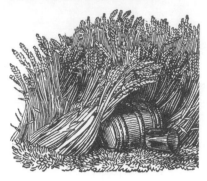

French Bread

1.5 LB (750 G)		
1 1/3 cups	water	325 mL
1 1/2 tsp	salt	7 mL
1 tbsp	granulated sugar	15 mL
3 2/3 cups	all-purpose flour or bread flour	825 mL
1 1/4 tsp	bread machine yeast	6 mL

2 LB (1 KG)		L
1 1/2 cups	water	350 mL
1 1/2 tsp	salt	7 mL
2 tbsp	granulated sugar	25 mL
4 cups	all-purpose flour or bread flour	950 mL
1 1/4 tsp	bread machine yeast	6 mL

1. Measure ingredients into baking pan in the order recommended by the manufacturer. Insert pan into the oven chamber.
2. Select **French Cycle**.

Enjoy the crisp crust and traditional texture of French bread for your dinner. No need to fuss with shaping it into a stick.

TIP

If your bread machine doesn't have a French Cycle, bake on the Basic Cycle with a dark crust setting.

When finished baking, remove immediately and serve the same day. Store in a paper bag, not plastic, to retain a crisp crust.

VARIATION

Add 2 tbsp (25 mL) dried onion flakes for a French Onion Bread.

Italian Herb Bread

1.5 LB (750 G)		
1 1/4 cups	water	300 mL
1/4 cup	skim milk powder	50 mL
1 tsp	salt	5 mL
1 tbsp	granulated sugar	15 mL
1 tbsp	shortening	15 mL
3 1/3 cups	all-purpose flour or bread flour	825 mL
1/4 cup	snipped fresh parsley	50 mL
1 tsp	dried basil	5 mL
1 tsp	dried marjoram	5 mL
1 tsp	dried thyme	5 mL
1 tsp	bread machine yeast	5 mL

2 LB (1 KG)		L
1 1/2 cups	water	350 mL
1/4 cup	skim milk powder	50 mL
1 1/2 tsp	salt	7 mL
2 tbsp	granulated sugar	25 mL
2 tbsp	shortening	25 mL
4 cups	all-purpose flour or bread flour	1 L
1/3 cup	snipped fresh parsley	75 mL
1 1/4 tsp	dried basil	6 mL
1 1/4 tsp	dried marjoram	6 mL
1 1/4 tsp	dried thyme	6 mL
1 1/4 tsp	bread machine yeast	6 mL

The fragrant aroma of this loaf makes waiting to eat extremely difficult. Serve this zesty herb bread with any course — soup, salad or entrée.

TIP

Wash and dry the fresh herbs thoroughly before snipping with scissors. Pack firmly to measure.

VARIATION

Croutons made from this loaf complement any salad. Cut leftover bread into 1/2-inch (1 cm) cubes, toss with melted butter and toast until crisp and lightly browned.

1. Measure ingredients into baking pan in the order recommended by the manufacturer. Insert pan into the oven chamber.
2. Select **Basic Cycle**.

Potato Chive Bread

1.5 LB (750 G)		
1 1/3 cups	water	325 mL
1/4 cup	skim milk powder	50 mL
1 1/4 tsp	salt	6 mL
1 tbsp	granulated sugar	15 mL
1 tbsp	vegetable oil	15 mL
3 1/4 cups	all-purpose flour or bread flour	800 mL
1/3 cup	instant potato flakes	75 mL
1/4 cup	snipped fresh parsley	50 mL
1/3 cup	snipped fresh chives	75 mL
2 tsp	bread machine yeast	10 mL

2 LB (1 KG)		
1 1/2 cups	water	375 mL
1/4 cup	skim milk powder	50 mL
1 1/2 tsp	salt	7 mL
2 tbsp	granulated sugar	25 mL
1 tbsp	vegetable oil	15 mL
3 1/4 cups	all-purpose flour or bread flour	800 mL
1/2 cup	instant potato flakes	125 mL
1/3 cup	snipped fresh parsley	75 mL
2/3 cup	snipped fresh chives	150 mL
2 tsp	bread machine yeast	10 mL

This mild-flavored, even-textured loaf has been a baker's favorite for generations.

TIP

Use 2 tbsp (25 mL) dried chives for 1/3 cup (75 mL) fresh and 1/4 cup (50 mL) dried for 2/3 cup (150 mL) fresh chives.

VARIATION

Substitute mashed potatoes for the potato flakes. Do not add milk or butter when mashing the potatoes. Decrease the water by 2 tbsp (25 mL).

1. Measure ingredients into baking pan in the order recommended by the manufacturer. Insert pan into the oven chamber.
2. Select **Quick Cycle**.

Seven-Grain Goodness Bread

1.5 LB (750 G)		
1 cup	unsweetened apple juice	250 mL
1/3 cup	unsweetened applesauce	75 mL
1 1/4 tsp	salt	6 mL
2 tbsp	honey	25 mL
1 tbsp	shortening	15 mL
1 cup	whole wheat flour	250 mL
2 cups	all-purpose flour or bread flour	500 mL
1/2 cup	7-grain cereal	125 mL
1/3 cup	buttermilk powder	75 mL
1 1/2 tsp	bread machine yeast	7 mL

2 LB (1 KG)		
1 1/4 cups	unsweetened apple juice	300 mL
1/2 cup	unsweetened applesauce	125 mL
1 1/2 tsp	salt	7 mL
2 tbsp	honey	25 mL
1 tbsp	shortening	15 mL
1 1/2 cups	whole wheat flour	375 mL
2 cups	all-purpose flour or bread flour	500 mL
3/4 cup	7-grain cereal	175 mL
1/2 cup	buttermilk powder	125 mL
1 3/4 tsp	bread machine yeast	8 mL

1. Measure ingredients into baking pan in the order recommended by the manufacturer. Insert pan into the oven chamber.
2. Select **Whole Wheat Cycle**.

Did you know there are eight ingredients in seven-grain cereal? Just imagine the texture and flavor of barley flakes, triticale flour, corn flakes, steel cut oats, rye meal, cracked wheat, flax seed and hulled millet.

TIP

Add applesauce and apple juice at room temperature for a lighter textured, higher loaf.

Store grains in an airtight container in the refrigerator or freezer and only purchase the amount to use within 3 months.

VARIATION

Substitute 3-, 5-, 9- or 12-grain cereals.

Vegetable Tarragon Wheat Bread

Fresh tarragon gives this loaf its sweet flavor.

TIP

If fresh tarragon is unavailable, use 2 to 3 tsp (10 to 15 mL) dried tarragon leaves.

Use an individual-serving size of instant vegetable soup mix.

VARIATION

Substitute basil for the tarragon. It makes an equally delicious loaf. For a more subtle flavor, use dill or parsley.

1.5 LB (750 G)		
1 cup	water	250 mL
1/4 tsp	orange extract	1 mL
1/4 cup	skim milk powder	50 mL
1 1/4 tsp	salt	6 mL
2 tbsp	honey	25 mL
1 tbsp	vegetable oil	15 mL
1 cup	whole wheat flour	250 mL
1 3/4 cups	all-purpose flour or bread flour	425 mL
1/2 cup	cracked wheat	125 mL
3/4 cup	shredded carrots	175 mL
2 tbsp	vegetable soup mix	25 mL
2 tbsp	fresh tarragon	25 mL
2 tsp	orange zest	10 mL
1 1/2 tsp	bread machine yeast	7 mL

2 LB (1 KG)		
1 1/3 cups	water	325 mL
1/4 tsp	orange extract	1 mL
1/4 cup	skim milk powder	50 mL
1 1/4 tsp	salt	6 mL
2 tbsp	honey	25 mL
1 tbsp	vegetable oil	15 mL
1 1/4 cups	whole wheat flour	300 mL
2 1/4 cups	all-purpose flour or bread flour	550 mL
3/4 cup	cracked wheat	175 mL
1 cup	shredded carrots	250 mL
3 tbsp	fresh tarragon	45 mL
3 tbsp	vegetable soup mix	45 mL
2 tsp	orange zest	10 mL
1 1/2 tsp	bread machine yeast	7 mL

1. Measure ingredients into baking pan in the order recommended by the manufacturer. Insert pan into the oven chamber.
2. Select **Whole Wheat Cycle**.

Lowering the fat without losing the flavor

1. Substitute lower-fat cheeses, adding a dash of dry mustard in cheese breads.
2. Replace sour cream with low-fat yogurt.
3. Use 2 egg whites instead of a whole egg.
4. Substitute raisins, dried apricots, figs or dates for nuts and seeds.
5. Replace 1 cup (250 mL) whole milk with 1/3 cup (75 mL) buttermilk powder and 1 cup (250 mL) water.
6. Spray baking pans with nonstick cooking spray instead of greasing with shortening, butter or margarine.
7. Replace the fat in the recipe with 1/2 cup (125 mL) applesauce.
8. Top bread slices with jam or low-fat spreads instead of butter or margarine.

Yummy Yogurt Dill Loaf

1.5 LB (750 G)		
1/4 cup	water	50 mL
1 cup	low-fat yogurt	250 mL
2	egg whites	2
1 1/2 tsp	salt	7 mL
3 tbsp	granulated sugar	45 mL
1 tbsp	vegetable oil	15 mL
3 1/3 cups	all-purpose flour or bread flour	825 mL
2 tbsp	minced dried onion	25 mL
1 tbsp	dried dill	15 mL
1 1/2 tsp	bread machine yeast	7 mL

2 LB (1 KG)		L
1/4 cup	water	50 mL
1 1/4 cups	low-fat yogurt	300 mL
3	egg whites	3
1 1/2 tsp	salt	7 mL
3 tbsp	granulated sugar	45 mL
1 tbsp	vegetable oil	15 mL
3 1/2 cups	all-purpose flour or bread flour	875 mL
3 tbsp	minced dried onion	45 mL
1 tbsp	dried dill	15 mL
1 1/2 tsp	bread machine yeast	7 mL

A delicious low-fat loaf flavored with dill and onion. The aroma as it bakes is tantalising.

TIP

Choose unflavored low-fat yogurt for this recipe.

VARIATION

Add zip by substituting fresh coriander and a dash of hot pepper sauce for the dill.

1. Measure ingredients into baking pan in the order recommended by the manufacturer. Insert pan into the oven chamber.
2. Select **Basic Cycle**.

WRAPS AND FLATBREADS

Today's busy lifestyle means most of us eat on the run. With your bread machine preparing the dough for these wraps and flatbreads, your life will be less complicated.

Make a meal or a snack for hungry teens with filled breads, or serve with a salad on a busy Friday night. These recipes will be a hit with your family. Let them choose and help prepare the toppings.

Beaver Tails

Served warm, these rich sweet treats have become a must-have during the winter. Beaver tails, as they are called in Canada, are similar to the American bear claw or elephant ear.

TIP

Stretch dough gently over your fingertips. The edges will be slightly thicker.

MAKES 10		

Preheat oil in deep-fryer to 350° F (180° C)

1 cup	milk	250 mL
1	egg	1
3/4 tsp	salt	4 mL
3 tbsp.	granulated sugar	40 mL
1 tbsp	butter	15 mL
3 1/4 cups	all-purpose flour or bread flour	800 mL
3/4 tsp	bread machine yeast	4 mL

1. Measure ingredients into baking pan in the order recommended by the manufacturer. Insert pan into the oven chamber. Select **Dough Cycle**.

2. Remove dough to a lightly floured surface; cover with a large bowl and let rest for 10 to 15 minutes. Divide the dough into 10 pieces. Gently stretch into 8- by 6-inch (20 by 15 cm) ovals.

3. Deep-fry for 30 to 45 seconds, holding the beaver tails under the fat until lightly browned, turning once. Drain well on paper towels.

4. Top the warm beaver tails with 1 to 2 tbsp (15 to 25 mL) of your choice of topping.

SUGGESTED TOPPINGS

Try your own favorite topping or one of the suggestions listed below:

- Sugar and cinnamon
- Sausage
- Cream cheese and green onion
- Jam
- Apple and cinnamon
- Chocolate and hazelnut
- Killaloe sunrise (sugar, cinnamon and lemon)
- Maple butter

Bruschetta
Basic Dough

MAKES 2 LOAVES

Preheat oven to 375° F (180° C)
Baking sheet, sprinkled with cornmeal

1 1/4 cups	water	300 mL
1 tsp	salt	5 mL
2 tsp	granulated sugar	10 mL
3 1/2 cups	all-purpose flour or bread flour	875 mL
1 1/2 tsp	bread machine yeast	7 mL
1	egg white	1
1 tbsp	water	15 mL

Begin with this baguette recipe. Prepare it early in the day and cool completely.

1. Measure the water, salt, sugar, flour and yeast into baking pan in the order recommended by the manufacturer. Insert pan into the oven chamber. Select **Dough Cycle**.

2. Remove dough to a lightly floured board; cover with a large bowl and let rest for 10 to 15 minutes. Divide the dough in half; form each into a long, thin rope, 1 inch (2.5 cm) in diameter and 16 inches (40 cm) long. (Loaves should be thicker in the middle and tapered at the ends.) Place on prepared baking sheet; cover and let dough rise in a warm, draft-free place for 30 to 45 minutes, or until doubled in volume.

3. Make 3 to 5 diagonal slits, 1/8 inch (2 mm) deep across the top of each loaf. Brush with the egg white beaten with water. Bake in preheated oven for 30 minutes or until loaves sound hollow when tapped on the bottom. For a crispier crust, place a pan of hot water in the oven and spritz the loaves with water every 5 to 10 minutes during baking.

4. Diagonally slice each loaf into 1-inch (2.5 cm) thick slices, toast one side, and top the untoasted side with your favorite bruschetta mixture. Three of our favorites are presented on the next few pages.

Enjoy the late-summer crop of fresh tomatoes with fresh basil from your garden in this delicious topping.

TIP

Choose a meaty plum tomato such as Roma or San Marzone.

To snip basil, place in a cup and cut with kitchen shears. Pack tightly to measure. If the flavor is too strong, use half basil and half parsley.

VARIATION

Substitute an equal amount of oregano or thyme for the basil.

A tasty bread to complement a vegetable stir-fry.

TIP

Preheat broiler for 8 to 10 minutes to quickly melt the cheese rather than bake it.

VARIATION

Try a Havarti and goat cheese combination and grill on the barbecue.

Fresh Tomato Basil Topping

MAKES ENOUGH FOR **16** SLICES		
Preheat broiler		
2 tbsp	extra virgin olive oil	25 mL
2	cloves minced garlic	2
4	chopped ripe tomatoes	4
1 tbsp	snipped fresh basil	15 mL
1/2 cup	grated mozzarella cheese	125 mL
1/4 cup	chopped fresh parsley	50 mL
1	baguette, diagonally sliced 1 inch (2.5 cm) thick, toasted on one side	1

1. Brush olive oil on the toasted 1-inch (2.5 cm) thick diagonal slices of baguette. Sprinkle with the remaining ingredients. Toast under the broiler just until the cheese melts.

Mozzarella Toast

MAKES ENOUGH FOR **16** SLICES		
Preheat broiler		
1/3 cup	softened butter	75 mL
6	minced anchovy fillets	6
2	cloves minced garlic	2
1/3 cup	grated mozzarella cheese	75 mL
1 to 2 tsp	dried basil	5 to 10 mL
1	baguette, diagonally sliced 1 inch (2.5 cm) thick, toasted on one side	1

1. In a bowl combine butter, anchovies and garlic. Spread mixture on untoasted side baguette slices. Sprinkle with cheese and top each with a pinch of basil. Toast under broiler just until the cheese melts.

Bright red peppers, piled high on each bruschetta slice, will whet the appetite of your guests at your next barbecue. The balsamic vinegar gives this colorful topping a rich, fruity character.

TIP

Place blistered roasted red peppers in a paper bag for 10 to 15 minutes, then peel. The skin will slip off easily.

VARIATION

Substitute yellow and orange bell peppers for an interesting color combination.

Roasted Red Pepper with Shrimp and Garlic

MAKES ENOUGH FOR **16** SLICES		
4	roasted chopped red bell peppers	4
48	cooked salad shrimp	48
1	clove minced garlic	1
1/2 cup	chopped fresh parsley	125 mL
2 tbsp	balsamic vinegar	25 mL
2 tsp	olive oil	10 mL
	freshly ground pepper	
1	baguette, diagonally sliced 1 inch (2.5 cm) thick, toasted on one side	1

1. To roast peppers: Place seeded pepper halves, skin-side up on a baking sheet. Bake at 375° F (190° C) for 30 to 45 minutes or until the skins are well blistered. Place peppers in a paper or plastic bag; seal well and set aside for 10 to 15 minutes. Remove from bag; the skins will loosen and peel easily.

2. In a bowl combine garlic, parsley, balsamic vinegar and olive oil; toss lightly. Season with pepper to taste. Add the mixture to the roasted peppers. Toss gently.

3. Heap mixture onto untoasted side of baguette slices. Top each with 3 shrimp.

Calzone

MAKES 10 CALZONE		
Preheat oven to 375° F (180° C)		
1 1/2 cups	water	375 mL
1/4 cup	skim milk powder	50 mL
1 1/2 tsp	salt	7 mL
2 tbsp	granulated sugar	25 mL
3 tbsp	shortening	45 mL
3 2/3 cups	all-purpose flour or bread flour	875 mL
1 tsp	bread machine yeast	5 mL

1. Measure ingredients into baking pan in the order recommended by the manufacturer. Insert pan into the oven chamber. Select **Dough Cycle**.

2. Remove the dough to a lightly floured board. Cover with a large bowl and let the dough rest for 10 to 15 minutes. Divide the dough into 10 portions. Roll out each into a 6-inch (15 cm) circle.

3. Prepare filling of your choice (recipes follow). Place filling on one-half of each circle. Fold in half, sealing the edges tightly. Cover and let rise in a warm, draft-free place until doubled in volume.

4. Bake in preheated oven for 20 to 25 minutes or until the calzone sound hollow when tapped on the bottom.

Ham and Swiss Cheese Filling

10 oz	sliced cooked ham	300 g
10 oz	sliced Swiss cheese	300 g

1. Cut ham and cheese slices into quarters. Place 4 quarters of each, alternating, on half of each circle of dough.

Perfect as a meal or snack for families on the go.

TIP

Make ahead, wrap individually and store in an airtight container in the refrigerator for a few days or in the freezer for up to one month.

VARIATION

For smaller cocktail-size calzone, divide dough into 20 portions and roll out each into a 3-inch (7.5 cm) circle. Use half the amount of filling for each. Bake for 15 to 20 minutes.

We had to include our families' favorite combo of ham and Swiss.

TIP

Cool slightly before serving; the cheese will be very hot!

VARIATION

Try leftover turkey and stuffing instead of ham.

Perfect as hors d'oeuvres. Serve piping hot. Your guests will rave.

TIP

No need to pre-cook these small florets of broccoli.

VARIATION

Try substituting feta cheese for the goat cheese and asparagus for the broccoli.

Decadently delicious, this updated version of cream cheese and lox filling combines goat cheese and smoked salmon.

TIP

Purchase pre-sliced smoked salmon or slice as thinly as possible.

VARIATION

Any soft unripened cheese, such as quark or ricotta, can be substituted. Don't forget the chopped onion and capers.

Broccoli and Goat Cheese Filling

2 to 3	sliced tomatoes	2 to 3
1 cup	broccoli florets	250 mL
3 to 4 oz	sliced goat cheese	90 to 120 g
2 tbsp	grated Parmesan cheese	25 mL
	Freshly ground pepper	
10	leaves fresh basil	10

1. Cover one half of each calzone with a thin slice of tomato, 2 to 3 broccoli florets, a thin slice of goat cheese, 1/2 tsp (2 mL) Parmesan cheese, a generous grind of black pepper and a fresh basil leaf.

Smoked Salmon Filling

1 lb	thinly sliced smoked salmon	500 g
8 oz	goat cheese *or* cream cheese	250 g
2 tbsp	finely chopped red onion	25 mL
2 tbsp	capers	25 mL

1. Cover one half of each calzone with salmon slices. Top with the remaining ingredients, dividing equally.

Ciabatta

From the Italian for "old slipper," ciabatta are flat, chewy loaves that are fun to make. Poke them full of dimples, both before and after rising. The flour-coated crust provides an interesting texture.

TIP

When dusting with flour, do not use any other finish or the crust will be sticky. Use a flour sifter for a light, even dusting.

VARIATION

Dust with rice or rye flour for an interesting flavor boost.

MAKES 2 CIABATTA		

Preheat oven to 425° F (220° C)
Baking sheet, lightly floured

1 1/2 cups	water	375 mL
1 1/2 tsp	salt	7 mL
1 tsp	granulated sugar	5 mL
1 tbsp	olive oil	15 mL
3 1/4 cups	all-purpose flour or bread flour	800 mL
1 1/2 tsp	bread machine yeast	7 mL

1. Measure ingredients into baking pan in the order recommended by the manufacturer. Insert pan into the oven chamber. Select **Dough Cycle**.

2. Remove dough to a lightly floured board. (This is a very sticky and moist dough, but resist the urge to add more flour). Cover with a large bowl and let the dough rest for 10 to 15 minutes. Divide the dough into half. Form each into a 13- by 4-inch (32.5 by 10 cm) oval. Place on prepared baking sheet. With floured fingers, make deep indentations all over each loaf making sure to press all the way down to the baking sheet. Dust the ovals lightly with flour.

3. Cover and allow to rise in a warm, draft-free place for 30 to 45 minutes or until doubled in volume. Make indents a second time.

4. Bake on the middle rack in preheated oven for 25 to 30 minutes or until the bread sounds hollow when tapped on bottom. For a crispier crust, put 12 ice cubes into a 13- by 9-inch (3 L) metal baking pan on bottom oven rack. During baking, spritz loaves with water every 5 to 10 minutes.

Crunchy Cheese-Filled Pretzels

MAKES **8** PRETZELS		

Preheat oven to 400° F (200° C)
Baking sheet, lightly greased

1 cup	beer	250 mL
1 tsp	salt	5 mL
2 tbsp	granulated sugar	25 mL
1 tbsp	butter	15 mL
2 3/4 cups	all-purpose flour or bread flour	675 mL
3/4 tsp	bread machine yeast	4 mL

Cheese Filling

1 2/3 cups	grated Cheddar cheese	400 mL
1/3 cup	chopped fresh parsley	75 mL
2 tbsp	Dijon mustard	25 mL
1/2 tsp	cracked peppercorns	2 mL

A little bit more work than some recipes, but definitely worth it. Your family will request encores of this tangy cheese treat.

TIP

Water can be substituted for beer; and Swiss, Havarti or mozzarella cheese for Cheddar cheese.

VARIATION

To spice up the filling, use an extra-old sharp Cheddar cheese and a few drops of hot pepper sauce or a pinch of cayenne pepper.

Topping

Brush with 1 egg white beaten with 1 tbsp (15 mL) water. Sprinkle with sea salt, coarse salt or poppy seeds.

1. Measure ingredients into baking pan in the order recommended by the manufacturer. Insert pan into the oven chamber. Select **Dough Cycle**.

2. Meanwhile prepare the cheese filling: In a bowl combine filling ingredients until crumbly; set aside.

3. Remove dough to a lightly floured board; cover with a large bowl and let rest for 10 to 15 minutes. Roll out the dough to a 10- by 16-inch (25 by 40 cm) rectangle. Cut lengthwise into 8 strips. Brush one long edge of each strip with water. Spread 1/4 cup (50 mL) filling down the center of each strip to within 1/2 inch (1 cm) of the ends and edges. Pinch the dough together. On a floured board, roll into a smooth rope, stretching to 16 inches (40 cm) long. Grasp the ends and twist into a rounded heart, at the same time moving to a greased baking sheet. Lightly press the ends into the curved part.

4. Cover and allow to rise in a warm, draft-free place for 1 hour or until doubled in volume.

5. Brush on the topping (see note, at left). Bake in preheated oven for 18 to 20 minutes or until pretzel sounds hollow when tapped on the bottom. Cool for 5 minutes. Remove to a rack to cool.

English Muffins

MAKES 24 ENGLISH MUFFINS		

Preheat grill to 500° F (260° C)
Baking sheet, sprinkled with cornmeal

1 cup	milk	250 mL
2	eggs	2
1 tsp	salt	5 mL
2 tbsp	granulated sugar	25 mL
2 tbsp	shortening	25 mL
3 cups	all-purpose flour or bread flour	750 mL
1 1/4 tsp	bread machine yeast	6 mL
	Cornmeal for topping	

A popular breakfast or brunch treat, just split with a fork and toast.

TIP

Follow the directions when rolling out the dough. If too thick, the muffins will brown before cooking through. Turn just once but do not press or flatten the tops.

VARIATION

Try substituting 1 cup (250 mL) whole wheat flour for 1 cup (250 mL) of all-purpose or bread flour.

1. Measure all ingredients *except the cornmeal* into baking pan in the order recommended by the manufacturer. Insert pan into the oven chamber. Select **Dough Cycle**.

2. Remove dough to a lightly floured board; cover with a large bowl and let rest for 10 to 15 minutes. Roll out dough to 1/4-inch (5 mm) thickness. Cut into 3-inch (7.5 cm) circles. Place on prepared baking sheet. Brush with water and sprinkle tops with cornmeal. Cover and allow to rise in a warm, draft-free place for 30 to 45 minutes or until doubled in volume.

3. Grill for 6 to 7 minutes on each side or until golden brown.

Greek-Style Pita

MAKES 12 PITAS		

Preheat oven to 450° F (230° C)
Preheated baking stone *or* baking sheet

1 1/4 cups	water	300 mL
1	egg	1
1 1/2 tsp	salt	7 mL
2 tsp	granulated sugar	10 mL
2 tbsp	shortening	25 mL
3 3/4 cups	all-purpose flour or bread flour	925 mL
1/2 cup	buttermilk powder	125 mL
1 1/2 tsp	bread machine yeast	7 mL

Greek-style pitas do not puff up to form a pocket. Spread with your favorite filling and roll for a quick portable lunch.

TIP

Steam finished pitas in foil to warm and soften before filling.

VARIATION

Form into large 8-inch (20 cm) circles, spread with cream cheese and thinly sliced deli meats. Roll tightly, slice diagonally and serve as hors d'oeuvres.

1. Measure ingredients into baking pan in the order recommended by the manufacturer. Insert pan into the oven chamber. Select **Dough Cycle**.

2. Remove dough to a lightly floured surface; cover with a large bowl and let rest for 10 to 15 minutes. Divide into 12 equal pieces and form into balls. Flatten each ball with your fingertips, working in as much flour as possible. Roll out into 7-inch (17.5 cm) circles, about 1/8 inch (2 mm) thick.

3. Quickly place 4 pitas on the hot baking stone. Bake in preheated oven for 3 minutes. For soft pitas, do not brown. Stack the pitas and immediately wrap in a lint-free towel to cool.

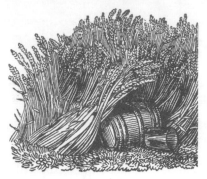

Focaccia

This slightly raised Italian flatbread has a pebbled, dimpled surface. Serve plain or in combination with your favorite fresh herbs, ripe olives or red onions.

Top focaccia with generous amounts of thinly sliced sweet onions, slowly cooked in a very small amount of olive oil until lightly golden.

TIP

No need for extra oil; keep onions covered and add 1 tbsp (15 mL) white wine or water to prevent sticking.

MAKES 2 FOCACCIA		

Preheat oven to 375° F (190° C)
Preheated baking stone *or* baking sheet, lightly greased

1 1/3 cups	water	325 mL
1 1/2 tsp	salt	7 mL
1 tsp	granulated sugar	5 mL
3 1/3 cups	all-purpose flour or bread flour	825 mL
2 1/4 tsp	bread machine yeast	11 mL

1. Measure ingredients into baking pan in the order recommended by the manufacturer. Insert pan into the oven chamber. Select **Dough Cycle**.
2. Remove dough to a lightly floured board; cover with a large bowl and let rest for 10 to 15 minutes.
3. Divide the dough in half. Stretch each half into a 10- by 8-inch (25 by 20 cm) rectangle. Dimple with flour-coated fingertips. Cover and let rise in a warm, draft-free place for 30 minutes. Re-dimple. Cover with preferred topping mixture (recipes follow).
4. Bake on the lowest rack of the preheated oven or hot baking stone for 20 to 30 minutes or until golden.

Caramelized Vidalia Onion Topping

2 tbsp	olive oil	25 mL
3 cups	sliced vidalia onions	750 mL
1 tbsp	balsamic vinegar	15 mL
8	sliced Kalamata olives	8
1/3 cup	crumbled feta cheese	75 mL
1 tbsp	snipped fresh thyme	15 mL

1. In a saucepan, heat oil over medium heat. Add onions and sauté until soft but not browned. Add vinegar and stir well. Spoon over prepared focaccia. Sprinkle remaining ingredients over the onions.

A trio of cheeses combined and sprinkled over a crisp focaccia — the perfect bread to accompany gazpacho on a hot summer's day.

TIP

Use the amounts of cheese stated in the recipe; too much will make the focaccia greasy.

VARIATION

Substitute cheeses with your favorite low-fat varieties.

Walnuts with freshly grated Parmesan cheese is a combination of flavors sure to please.

TIP

Store walnuts in the refrigerator and taste for freshness before using.

VARIATION

Pine nuts can be substituted for walnuts and Romano cheese for the Parmesan.

Triple-Cheese Topping

1 to 2 tbsp	olive oil	15 to 25 mL
2	cloves minced garlic	2
1 tsp	dried basil	5 mL
1/2 to 1 cup	prepared salsa	125 to 250 mL
1/2 cup	shredded Asiago cheese	125 mL
1/2 cup	shredded mozzarella cheese	125 mL
1/4 cup	grated Parmesan cheese	50 mL
	Salsa for garnish	

1. Mix together olive oil and garlic for a more even coverage. Drizzle over the dough; allow to puddle in the dimples. Top with basil and salsa. Mix the 3 cheeses together. Sprinkle over salsa.

Parmesan Walnut Topping

2 tbsp	olive oil	25 mL
2	cloves garlic, minced	2
1/2 cup	chopped walnuts	125 mL
2 tbsp	grated Parmesan cheese	25 mL

1. Mix together olive oil and garlic. Drizzle over the dough; allow to puddle in the dimples. Top the dough with walnuts and Parmesan cheese.

Indian Style Naan

MAKES 8 NAAN		

Preheat oven to 375° F (190° C)
Baking sheet, sprinkled with cornmeal

3/4 cup	water	175 mL
1/2 cup	yogurt	125 mL
1	egg yolk	1
1 1/2 tsp	salt	7 mL
1 tbsp	butter	15 mL
3 1/3 cups	all-purpose flour or bread flour	825 mL
1 1/2 tsp	baking powder	7 mL
1 1/2 tsp	bread machine yeast	7 mL

TOPPING		
2 tsp	melted butter	10 mL
2 tsp	sesame seeds *or* minced onion	10 mL

In India this golden puffed bread is served right off the sides of a tandoor oven. Naan is a must to accompany curry dishes.

TIP

Cool the melted butter slightly before brushing on the risen dough.

Bake these teardrop-shaped breads, just until lightly browned or they will toughen.

VARIATION

Grill on the barbecue over medium-high heat, directly on the grill rack, with the lid closed, for 3 to 4 minutes per side.

1. Measure ingredients into baking pan in the order recommended by the manufacturer. Insert pan into the oven chamber. Select **Dough Cycle**.

2. Remove dough to a lightly floured surface; cover with a large bowl and let rest for 10 to 15 minutes. Divide the dough into 8 pieces and roll into balls. Cover and let rest for 10 minutes. Gently stretch into a teardrop shape about 1/4 inch (5 mm) thick. Cover and let rest for 15 minutes.

3. Add topping: Brush the dough with melted butter. Sprinkle with sesame seeds or minced onion.

4. Bake in preheated oven for 8 to 10 minutes or until the naan sounds hollow when tapped on the bottom.

Lavosh Crisps with Sesame Seeds

MAKES 4 CRISPS		

Preheat oven to 375° F (190° C)
Preheated baking stone *or* baking sheet

1 1/4 cups	water	300 mL
1/4 cup	skim milk powder	50 mL
1 1/2 tsp	salt	7 mL
1 tsp	granulated sugar	5 mL
2 tbsp	shortening	25 mL
3 1/2 cups	all purpose flour or bread flour	875 mL
1 1/4 tsp	bread machine yeast	6 mL
1 cup	sesame seeds	250 mL

1. Measure all ingredients *except sesame seeds* into baking pan in the order recommended by the manufacturer. Insert pan into the oven chamber. Select **Dough Cycle**.

2. Remove dough to a lightly floured board; cover with a large bowl and let rest for 10 to 15 minutes. Divide into 4 equal portions. Spread 1/4 cup (50 mL) sesame seeds on the board. Roll one portion of dough as thinly as possible, turning over frequently to press the seeds into the dough. Repeat with the remaining portions.

3. Bake in preheated oven for 13 to 18 minutes until golden brown and large bubbles form. Remove from the oven; allow to cool and break into large pieces.

This thin, crisp Armenian flatbread is covered with sesame seeds, which toast as it bakes. Your guests will wonder how you prepared the crisps.

TIP

Store in an airtight container for up to 2 to 3 months. Crisp in the oven, if necessary, before serving.

The thinner the dough is rolled, the more authentic the bread will be.

VARIATION

Break this thin crunchy bread into crisps to serve with soups, salads or dips.

Make "bread bowls" by shaping the dough around a greased oven-proof bowl before baking. Remove carefully. To serve, fill with soup, chili or curry. Then eat the bowl!

Middle Eastern Flatbread

MAKES **8** FLATBREADS		

Preheat oven to 425° F (220° C)
Preheated baking stone *or* baking sheet

1 1/4 cups	water	300 mL
1/4 cup	skim milk powder	50 mL
1 1/2 tsp	salt	7 mL
1 tsp	honey	5 mL
2 tbsp	olive oil	25 mL
3 1/2 cups	all purpose flour or bread flour	875 mL
1 1/4 tsp	bread machine yeast	6 mL

TOPPING		
2 tbsp	olive oil	(25 mL)
1 tbsp	lemon juice	(15 mL)
2 tsp	Zahtar spice	(10 mL)

This bread complements a grilled salmon steak and a spicy corn and black bean salsa.

TIP

Quickly immerse this flatbread in water, blot dry and roll up jellyroll-style around deli meats for a delicious luncheon treat to go.

VARIATION

Grill the flatbread dough quickly on your outdoor barbecue. Place dough on 2 baking sheets stacked together, then cook on the grill. This will help to prevent burning.

1. Measure ingredients into baking pan in the order recommended by the manufacturer. Insert pan into the oven chamber. Select **Dough Cycle**.

2. Remove dough to a lightly floured board; cover with a large bowl and let rest for 10 to 15 minutes. Flatten dough into a circle. Cut into 8 wedges. Stretch each into a triangle 1/4 inch (5 mm) thick. Place on a baking sheet, cover and let rest for 15 minutes.

3. Topping: In a bowl combine all topping ingredients. Brush over each triangle.

4. Bake in preheated oven for 10 minutes or until golden brown.

Pita Pockets

Preheat oven to 450° F (230° C)
Preheated baking stone *or* baking sheet

1 1/4 cups	water	300 mL
1 1/2 tsp	salt	7 mL
1 tbsp	granulated sugar	15 mL
1/4 cup	shortening	50 mL
2 1/4 cups	all-purpose flour or bread flour	550 mL
1 cup	rye flour	250 mL
1/2 cup	buttermilk powder	125 mL
2 1/2 tsp	bread machine yeast	12 mL

Watch these pitas puff up in the oven right before your eyes.

TIP

Timing is critical in this recipe. Remove pitas from the oven before they begin to brown.

Work in as much flour as possible with your hand as you form these pitas. This gives the typical texture and makes separating them into pockets easier.

VARIATION

Try making pita crisps. Separate pita layers by cutting or pulling apart. Cut both circles into 4 or 8 wedges. (The number depends on the size of each pita.) Bake, turning once, at 350° F (180° C) for 10 to 15 minutes or until lightly browned and crisp or broil 2 to 4 minutes until golden and crisp.

1. Measure ingredients into baking pan in the order recommended by the manufacturer. Insert pan into the oven chamber. Select **Dough Cycle**.

2. Remove dough to a lightly floured board; cover with a large bowl and let rest for 10 to 15 minutes. Divide the dough into 16 portions. Form into balls; flatten each with your fingertips, working in as much flour as possible. Roll out into 5-inch (12.5 cm) circles, 1/8 inch (2 mm) thick.

3. Place rack on bottom third of oven. Preheat unglazed baking tiles for 5 minutes in 450° F (230° C) oven. Quickly place 3 or 4 pitas on the preheated baking stone or baking sheet. Bake for 3 minutes. For soft pitas, do not brown. Immediately upon removing from the oven, stack the puffed pitas. Wrap in a towel while cooling. If the pitas are too thick, they may not form a pocket.

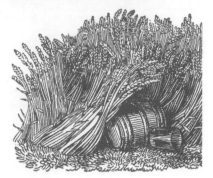

This tender, thin crust has an extra tang from the beer.

Beer Pizza Crust

**Makes two 12-inch (30 cm) thin pizzas
or one thicker 20- by 8-inch (50 by 20 cm) pizza
Preheat oven to 400° F (200° C)**

1 cup	beer	250 mL
1 tsp	salt	5 mL
2 tsp	granulated sugar	10 mL
3 cups	all-purpose flour or bread flour	750 mL
2 tsp	dried basil	10 mL
1 1/2 tsp	bread machine yeast	7 mL

1. Measure ingredients into baking pan in the order recommended by the manufacturer. Insert pan into the oven chamber. Select **Dough Cycle**.

2. Remove dough to a lightly floured board; cover with a large bowl and let rest for 10 to 15 minutes. Roll out dough or press into the pan.

3. To partially bake the pizza crust, bake in preheated oven for 10 to 12 minutes. Spread with your choice of topping (see suggestions, pages 59-60).

Herb Pizza Crust

Makes two 12-inch (30 cm) thin pizzas
***or* one thicker 20- by 8-inch (50 by 20 cm) pizza**
Preheat oven to 400° F (200° C)

1 cup	water	250 mL
1 tsp	salt	5 mL
1 tbsp	granulated sugar	15 mL
2 3/4 cups	all-purpose flour or bread flour	675 mL
1 tsp	dried basil	5 mL
1 tsp	dried oregano	5 mL
1 1/4 tsp	bread machine yeast	6 mL

1. Measure ingredients into baking pan in the order recommended by the manufacturer. Insert pan into the oven chamber. Select **Dough Cycle**.
2. Remove dough to a lightly floured board; cover with a large bowl and let rest for 10 to 15 minutes. Roll out dough or press into the pan.
3. To partially bake the pizza crust, bake in the preheated oven for 10 to 12 minutes. Spread with your choice of topping (recipes follow).

Leek and Mushroom with Asiago Cheese Topping

3 tbsp	olive oil	45 mL
1	clove minced garlic	1
4 cups	sliced cremini mushrooms	1 L
5 cups	sliced leeks	1.25 L
2/3 cup	crumbled Asiago cheese	150 mL
2/3 cup	grated old Cheddar cheese	150 mL

1. In a saucepan, heat oil over medium heat. Add garlic, mushrooms and leeks; cook until tender. Spread vegetables over partially baked pizza crust. Top with the cheeses. Bake at 400° F (200° C) for 15 to 20 minutes or until firm.

According to the topping chosen, select different herbs: oregano for vegetarian, basil for Mediterranean, or fresh rosemary for the milder flavored leek and mushroom.

TIP

Use only the white part of the leeks. Slice lengthwise and hold under cold running water to clean out any dirt.

The pan and oil must be hot before adding the mushrooms to sauté.

VARIATION

Select a meatier-textured variety of mushroom such as cremini, portobello or shiitake.

Ripe tomatoes, sliced black olives, fresh oregano and crumbled feta cheese. This pizza zings with the flavors of the Mediterranean.

TIP

Drain the feta well before using.

VARIATION

Although black olives are the traditional choice, here feel free to substitute green olives.

Here's a great way to use up leftover vegetables! Try mushrooms, broccoli, onions, snow peas, artichokes, tomatoes, and roasted peppers.

TIP

Add a bit of crumbled firm tofu or tofu cheese in place of the mozzarella.

VARIATION

For a new treat, try topping the pizza with blanched green beans or asparagus, sliced cooked potatoes and Spanish onions.

Mediterranean Topping

3 tbsp	pasta sauce	45 mL
1 cup	grilled zucchini slices	250 mL
3 to 4	grilled eggplant slices	3 to 4
1 cup	grilled shiitake mushrooms	250 mL
1/2 cup	chopped roasted red pepper	125 mL
3	chopped fresh basil leaves	3
1 cup	shredded mozzarella cheese	250 mL
1/4 cup	crumbled feta cheese	50 mL

1. Spread the spaghetti sauce onto the partially baked pizza crust. Top with the vegetables, basil and cheeses. Bake at 400° F (200° C) for 15 to 20 minutes or until firm.

Vegetarian Topping

3 tbsp	olive oil	45 mL
1 tbsp	minced garlic	15 mL
2	sliced tomatoes	2
1/2 cup	thinly sliced onions	125 mL
1 1/2 cups	sliced cremini mushrooms	375 mL
1	thinly sliced red bell pepper	1
1 cup	broccoli florets	250 mL
1 cup	grated mozzarella cheese	250 mL
1/2 cup	freshly grated Parmesan cheese	125 mL

1. Brush partially baked pizza crust with olive oil. Sprinkle with garlic. Arrange tomatoes, onions, mushrooms, red pepper and broccoli over top. Sprinkle with cheeses. Bake at 400° F (200° C) for 15 to 20 minutes or until firm.

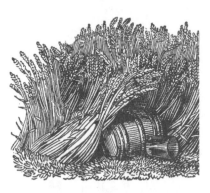

Spinach Feta Twist

BREAD (MAKES 1 TWIST)		
Tube pan, lightly greased		
1 cup	water	250 mL
1/2 cup	crumbled feta cheese	125 mL
1	egg	1
1 1/2 tsp	salt	7 mL
2 tbsp	olive oil	25 mL
3 3/4 cups	all-purpose flour or bread flour	925 mL
1 1/4 tsp	bread machine yeast	6 mL

SPINACH FILLING		
10 oz	fresh spinach	300 g
1 tbsp	melted butter	15 mL
1	clove garlic, minced	1
1/4 cup	grated Parmesan cheese	50 mL
2 tsp	dried oregano	10 mL
1/2 cup	crumbled feta cheese	125 mL
1/4 cup	sliced Kalamata olives	50 mL

TOPPING		
1	egg white	1
1 tbsp	water	15 mL
1 tbsp	grated Parmesan cheese	15 mL

For a Greek luncheon treat, cut this twist into thick wedges, add a fresh salad and the menu is complete.

TIP

Be sure to squeeze the moisture out of the spinach before measuring.

VARIATION

An equal amount of frozen, thawed spinach can be substituted for the fresh.

1. Measure ingredients into baking pan in the order recommended by the manufacturer. Insert pan into the oven chamber. Select **Dough Cycle**.

2. Meanwhile, prepare the spinach filling: Wash spinach, shaking off the excess water. Remove stems. Wilt in microwave, uncovered, at High for 2 to 3 minutes, stirring at half time. Squeeze out the excess moisture and allow to cool.

3. In a medium bowl, gently mix together the spinach, butter, garlic, Parmesan cheese and oregano.

Recipe continues next page…

4. Remove dough to a lightly floured board; cover with a large bowl and let rest for 10 to 15 minutes. Roll out to an 18- by 15-inch (45 by 38 cm) rectangle.

5. Spread filling on dough to within 1/2 inch (1 cm) of the edges. Sprinkle with feta cheese and Kalamata olives. Starting at long side, tightly roll up like a jellyroll. Pinch seams to seal. Cut in half lengthwise using scissors to prevent crushing. Twist the halves together, keeping cut sides up and filling visible (like twisting 2 strands of rope). Keeping the filling-side up, shape into a ring; placing in prepared tube pan.

6. Cover and allow to rise in a warm, draft-free place for 45 to 60 minutes or until doubled in volume. Brush with the egg white combined with water. Sprinkle with Parmesan cheese.

7. Bake at 375° F (190° C) for 45 to 55 minutes or until the bread sounds hollow when tapped on the bottom.

Easy baking tips for crisp crusts and focaccia

1. Use a baking stone
Baking stones, available in different sizes and shapes, are made of unglazed quarry or ceramic tile. Preheat on the bottom rack at least 10 to 15 minutes before using. Cooling completely, scrape off any burnt matter. Wipe the stone with a damp cloth. Use for Pitas, Pizza and Naan bread when a crisp crust is desired.

2. Use a peel
A peel is a wooden or metal long handled, thin, flat blade. Slide it under the risen dough or crust and ease it onto the baking stone or oven rack. A peel prevents the raw dough from wrinkling as you slide it into the oven and protects your fingers, preventing burns from the hot oven surfaces or the baking stone.

3. Cut with a pizza wheel
A pizza wheel has a sharpened stainless steel circular wheel anchored to a handle. Use it to cut dough for breadsticks, pizza or toasties.

4. Pre-bake pizza crusts
Bake shaped pizza crusts in a 450° F (220° C) oven for 12 to 15 minutes before adding the toppings. The crust will not become soggy and will bake without burning.

TANGY SOURDOUGHS

Sourdough baking can be a challenge, but the results are more than worth it. Begin by making the starter, then watch and stir it over the next week. Use part of the starter and "feed" the remainder to keep it alive and active.

STEPS TO SUCCESSFUL SOURDOUGH BAKING

1. Using the Starter

The starter should have the consistency of thin pancake batter. If too thick, add a small amount of water before measuring. If your bread machine does not have a 20- to 30-minute delay to preheat before mixing, bring the starter to room temperature or place in a bowl of warm water for 15 minutes before measuring. Until the starter becomes established and is working well, remove only 1 cup (250 mL) at a time.

2. Feeding the Starter

To replace each 1 cup (250 mL) of starter used in preparing a recipe, add 3/4 cup (175 mL) water, 3/4 cup (175 mL) flour and 1 tsp (5 mL) sugar. Stir well, using a wooden spoon, and let stand at room temperature for at least 24 hours or until bubbly.

3. Storing the Starter

Refrigerate, loosely covered, until needed. If not used regularly, stir in 1 tsp (5 mL) sugar every 10 days. The starter can be kept for years, shared with friends, or even passed from generation to generation!

SPINACH FETA TWIST (PAGE 61) ➢

OVERLEAF (CLOCKWISE FROM UPPER LEFT):
CARAMELIZED VIDALIA ONION FOCACCIA (PAGE 52);
TRIPLE-CHEESE FOCACCIA (PAGE 53); PARMESAN WALNUT FOCACCIA (PAGE 53)

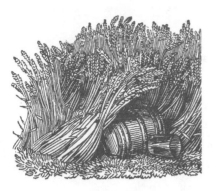

Sourdough Starter

MAKES ABOUT 3 CUPS (750 mL)		
1 1/4 tsp	yeast	6 mL
1/2 cup	warm water	125 mL
2 1/4 cups	warm water	300 mL
1 tbsp	granulated sugar	15 mL
2 cups	all-purpose flour or bread flour	500 mL

Prepare the starter at least 7 to 10 days before you plan to bake the sourdough bread.

TIP

If the starter liquid is green, pink or orange — or develops mold — throw it out and begin again.

Store prepared starter in a glass jar covered loosely with aluminum foil or a lid, partially screwed on to allow gases to escape.

1. In a large glass bowl, sprinkle yeast over 1/2 cup (125 mL) warm water. Let stand for 10 minutes. Add remaining 2 1/4 cups (300 mL) warm water, sugar and flour; beat until smooth.

2. Cover bowl with a layer of cheesecloth and let stand at room temperature for 5 to 10 days, stirring with a wooden spoon 2 or 3 times a day. When ready to use, the starter has a sour smell with small bubbles on (or rising to) the surface.

◄ SOURDOUGH PUMPERNICKEL RAISIN BREAD (PAGE 68)

Sourdough Cornmeal Bread

1 cup	SOURDOUGH STARTER (see recipe, page 65)	250 mL
1/2 cup	water	125 mL
1	egg	1
1/4 cup	skim milk powder	50 mL
1 1/2 tsp	salt	8 mL
2 tbsp	honey	25 mL
2 tbsp	shortening	25 mL
3 1/4 cups	all-purpose flour or bread flour	800 mL
1/3 cup	cornmeal	75 mL
1 tsp	bread machine yeast	5 mL

1. Measure ingredients into baking pan in the order recommended by the manufacturer. Insert pan into the oven chamber.
2. Select **Basic Cycle**.

A good old Southern favorite, this bread has a tangy flavor and tuggy texture.

TIP

Because of the egg and the starter in this loaf, you should not use the timer on your machine.

VARIATION

We use a medium-grind yellow cornmeal, however blue or white can be substituted.

This delightfully tangy loaf has the crunchy texture and natural whole-grain goodness of cracked wheat.

TIP

Be sure the cracked wheat is not touching water when using the timer or the loaf may be short and heavy.

VARIATION

Bulgur can be substituted for the cracked wheat.

Sourdough Cracked Wheat Bread

1 cup	SOURDOUGH STARTER (see recipe, page 65)	250 mL
3/4 cup	water	175 mL
1/4 cup	skim milk powder	50 mL
1 1/2 tsp	salt	7 mL
3 tbsp	honey	45 mL
3 tbsp	shortening	45 mL
1 1/4 cups	whole wheat flour	300 mL
2 cups	all-purpose flour or bread flour	500 mL
3/4 cup	cracked wheat	175 mL
1 3/4 tsp	bread machine yeast	8 mL

1. Measure ingredients into baking pan in the order recommended by the manufacturer. Insert pan into the oven chamber.
2. Select **Whole Wheat Cycle**.

Sourdough Pumpernickel Raisin Bread

Your taste buds won't know what hit them when they experience the tang of sourdough combined with the sweetness of raisins and the savory flavor of pumpernickel.

TIP

Prepare this loaf for weekend lunches featuring grilled cheese sandwiches.

VARIATION

Add 2 tsp (10 mL) orange zest and 1/2 tsp (2 mL) ground anise seed for a more pronounced Scandinavian taste.

1 cup	SOURDOUGH STARTER (see recipe, page 65)	250 mL
3/4 cup	water	175 mL
2 tbsp	skim milk powder	25 mL
1 tsp	salt	5 mL
2 tbsp	honey	25 mL
2 tbsp	molasses	25 mL
2 tbsp	shortening	25 mL
3/4 cup	whole wheat flour	175 mL
1 3/4 cups	all-purpose flour or bread flour	425 mL
1/2 cup	rye flour	125 mL
2 tsp	cocoa	10 mL
1 tsp	instant coffee granules	5 mL
1 1/4 tsp	bread machine yeast	6 mL
1/3 cup	raisins	75 mL

1. Measure all ingredients *except raisins* into baking pan in the order recommended by the manufacturer. Insert pan into the oven chamber.
2. Select **Basic Cycle**.
3. Add raisins at the "add ingredient" signal.

Sourdough Rustic White Bread

1 cup	SOURDOUGH STARTER (see recipe, page 65)	250 mL
1/2 cup	water	125 mL
1/4 cup	skim milk powder	50 mL
1 1/4 tsp	salt	6 mL
2 tbsp	granulated sugar	25 mL
2 tbsp	shortening	25 mL
3 cups	all-purpose flour or bread flour	750 mL
1 1/4 tsp	bread machine yeast	6 mL

1. Measure ingredients into baking pan in the order recommended by the manufacturer. Insert pan into the oven chamber.
2. Select **Basic Cycle**.

Here's a definitive San Francisco-style sourdough. It has that characteristic tangy flavor and tuggy texture.

TIP

For a change in color and flavor, try making and/or feeding the starter with whole wheat rather than bread flour.

VARIATION

For a rustic brown bread, try using half whole wheat flour.

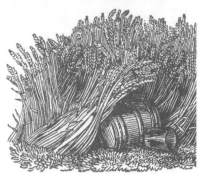

Sourdough Submarine Buns

MAKES 6 BUNS		

Preheat oven to 350° F (180° C)
Baking sheet, sprinkled with 1 to 2 tbsp (15 to 25 mL)
cornmeal

1 cup	SOURDOUGH STARTER (see recipe, page 65)	250 mL
3/4 cup	water	175 mL
1	egg	1
1 1/4 tsp	salt	6 mL
1 tbsp	granulated sugar	15 mL
3 1/2 cups	all-purpose flour or bread flour	875 mL
1 1/4 tsp	bread machine yeast	6 mL

TOPPING		
1	egg white	1
1 tbsp	water	15 mL

1. Measure ingredients into baking pan in the order recommended by the manufacturer. Insert pan into the oven chamber. Select **Dough Cycle**.

2. Remove dough to a lightly floured board; cover with a large bowl and let rest for 10 to 15 minutes. Divide into 6 portions. Shape into 12-inch (30 cm) long buns. Place on the prepared baking sheet.

3. Cover and let the dough rise in a warm, draft-free place for 30 to 45 minutes or until doubled in volume.

4. Brush with the egg white combined with water. Bake in preheated oven for 15 to 20 minutes or until the buns sound hollow when tapped on the bottom.

A touch of "sour" in these submarine buns complements spicy deli meats.

TIP

Younger children love these buns made in a smaller size — perfect for the lunch box (see below).

VARIATION

To make a smaller version, suitable for hamburger or hot dog buns, roll dough into 12 buns each 6 inches (15 cm) in length. Finish recipe as given.

MONTREAL-STYLE BAGELS

STEPS TO PERFECT BAGELS

1. Proofing

Cover and let dough rise in a warm, draft-free place for 30 to 45 minutes, or until doubled in volume. To test readiness, press two fingers into the dough. The indents should remain.

2. Boiling

It is important to boil bagels before baking to give a shiny appearance, to deactivate the yeast (by raising the internal temperatures to 130° F [55° C]), and to give the characteristic chewy texture and a thick, crisp crust.

Bring a large pot of water plus 1 tbsp (15 mL) sugar to a gentle yet full boil. Immerse bagels in water, one at a time, turning upside down. Hold under water for 20 seconds with a skimmer or large spoon until the dough becomes a little puffy. Remove and dip into a bowl of topping, if desired.

3. Baking

Sprinkle baking sheet with cornmeal or semolina flour rather than greasing it. Bake at 400° F (200° C) for 15 minutes or until the bagel sounds hollow when tapped on the bottom. Sweet or seed-topped bagels will brown quickly. Tent with foil to prevent burning. Remove the foil for the last 5 minutes to brown the bagels.

A pleasantly sweet butterscotch flavor combines with a nutty crunch in this low-fat dessert bagel.

TIP

To economize, purchase pecan pieces from the bulk store.

VARIATION

Substitute white or semi-sweet chocolate chips for butterscotch chips.

Butter Pecan Bagels

MAKES **8** BAGELS		

Preheat oven to 400° F (200° C)
Preheated baking stone *or* baking sheet, lightly greased

1 1/4 cups	water	300 mL
1 tsp	salt	5 mL
1/4 cup	packed brown sugar	50 mL
3 1/2 cups	all-purpose flour or bread flour	875 mL
1/2 cup	butterscotch chips	125 mL
1/2 cup	chopped pecans	125 mL
2 tsp	bread machine yeast	10 mL

1. Measure ingredients into baking pan in the order recommended by the manufacturer. Place pan into the oven chamber. Select **Dough Cycle**.

2. Remove dough to a lightly floured surface; cover with a large bowl and let rest for 10 to 15 minutes. Shape the dough into a round cylinder 12 inches (30 cm) long. Cut into 8 portions 1 1/2 inches (4 cm) wide. Push thumbs through the center of each piece and pull into a bagel shape, rounding all the surfaces.

3. Place dough on prepared baking sheet; cover and let rise in a warm, draft-free place for 30 to 45 minutes or until doubled in volume.

4. Bring a large pot of water and 1 tbsp (15 mL) sugar to a gentle yet full boil. Immerse the bagels in water one at a time, turning upside down. Hold under the water for 20 seconds with a skimmer or large spoon until the dough becomes a little puffy.

5. Bake on preheated baking stone or prepared baking sheet in preheated oven for 15 minutes or until the bagels sound hollow when tapped on the bottom.

Roasted onions top this savory cheese bagel.

TIP

Whole onions can be roasted on an outside or inside grill. The charred outer layer is easily removed by squeezing one end.

VARIATION

For a stronger cheese flavor, substitute 1/4 cup (50 mL) Romano cheese for the Parmesan and add 1/4 tsp (1 mL) dry mustard.

Cheese Onion Bagels

MAKES 8 BAGELS		

Preheat oven to 400° F (200° C)
Preheated baking stone *or* baking sheet, lightly greased

1 1/4 cups	water	300 mL
1 tsp	salt	5 mL
3 tbsp	granulated sugar	45 mL
3 1/2 cups	all-purpose flour or bread flour	875 mL
1/2 cup	grated old Cheddar cheese	125 mL
1/4 cup	grated Parmesan cheese	50 mL
2 tbsp	minced dried onion	25 mL
2 tsp	bread machine yeast	10 mL

1. Measure ingredients into baking pan in the order recommended by the manufacturer. Place pan in the oven chamber. Select **Dough Cycle**.

2. Remove dough to a lightly floured surface; cover with a large bowl and let rest for 10 to 15 minutes. Shape the dough into a round cylinder 12 inches (30 cm) long. Cut into 8 portions 1 1/2 inch (4 cm) wide. Push thumbs through the center of each piece and pull into a bagel shape, rounding all the surfaces.

3. Place dough on prepared baking sheet; cover and let rise in a warm, draft-free place for 30 to 45 minutes or until doubled in volume.

4. Bring a large pot of water and 1 tbsp (15 mL) sugar to a gentle yet full boil. Immerse bagels in water one at a time, turning upside down. Hold under the water for 20 seconds with a skimmer or large spoon until the dough becomes a little puffy. Top with roasted onions.

5. Bake on the preheated baking stone or prepared baking sheet in preheated oven for 15 minutes or until the bagels sound hollow when tapped on the bottom.

Mocha Bagels

MAKES 8 BAGELS		

Preheat oven to 400° F (200° C)
Preheated baking stone *or* baking sheet, lightly greased

1 1/4 cups	water	300 mL
1 tsp	salt	5 mL
1/4 cup	packed brown sugar	50 mL
3 1/2 cups	all-purpose flour or bread flour	875 mL
1/2 cup	chocolate chips	125 mL
1 tsp	instant coffee granules	5 mL
2 tsp	bread machine yeast	10 mL

Chocolate and coffee team together in this delicious treat.

TIP

An equal amount of cold leftover coffee can be substituted for the water and instant coffee granules.

VARIATION

Try your favorite flavored coffee, such as Irish Cream or French Vanilla, for a personalized treat.

1. Measure ingredients into baking pan in the order recommended by the manufacturer. Place pan in the oven chamber. Select **Dough Cycle**.

2. Remove dough to a lightly floured surface; cover with a large bowl and let rest for 10 to 15 minutes. Shape the dough into a round cylinder 12 inches (30 cm) long. Cut into 8 portions 1 1/2 inch (4 cm) wide. Push thumbs through the center of each piece and pull into a bagel shape, rounding all the surfaces.

3. Place dough on prepared baking sheet; cover and let rise in a warm, draft-free place for 30 to 45 minutes or until doubled in volume.

4. Bring a large pot of water and 1 tbsp (15 mL) sugar to a gentle yet full boil. Immerse bagels in water one at a time, turning upside down. Hold under the water for 20 seconds with a skimmer or large spoon until the dough becomes a little puffy.

5. Bake on the preheated baking stone or prepared baking sheet in preheated oven for 15 minutes or until the bagels sound hollow when tapped on the bottom.

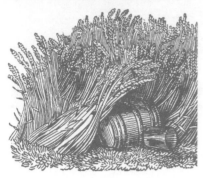

Muesli Bagels

Preheat oven to 400° F (200° C)
Preheated baking stone *or* baking sheet, lightly greased

1 1/4 cups	water	300 mL
1 tsp	salt	5 mL
2 tbsp	honey	25 mL
2 3/4 cups	all-purpose flour or bread flour	675 mL
1 cup	muesli	250 mL
1/2 cup	raw unsalted sunflower seeds	125 mL
2 tsp	bread machine yeast	10 mL

There's more crunch in every bite when you add a coat of muesli to the tops of these bagels.

TIP

Muesli is quite perishable, so purchase small quantities and store in the refrigerator.

Pre-packaged boxed Muesli cereals contain extra fat and sugar and may result in a completely different bagel. Choose lower-fat unsweetened varieties.

VARIATION

Add 1/4 cup (50 mL) each raisins and sunflower seeds.

1. Measure ingredients into baking pan in the order recommended by the manufacturer. Place in the oven chamber. Select **Dough Cycle**.

2. Remove dough to a lightly floured surface; cover with a large bowl and let rest for 10 to 15 minutes. Shape the dough into a round cylinder 12 inches (30 cm) long. Cut into 8 portions 1 1/2 inch (4 cm) wide. Push thumbs through the center of each piece and pull into a bagel shape, rounding all the surfaces.

3. Place dough on prepared baking sheet; cover and let rise in a warm, draft-free place for 30 to 45 minutes or until doubled in volume.

4. Bring a large pot of water and 1 tbsp (15 mL) sugar to a gentle yet full boil. Immerse bagels in water one at a time, turning upside down. Hold under the water for 20 seconds with a skimmer or large spoon until the dough becomes a little puffy.

5. Bake on the preheated baking stone or prepared baking sheet in preheated oven for 15 minutes or until the bagels sound hollow when tapped on the bottom.

Roasted Garlic Bagels

MAKES 8 BAGELS		

Preheat oven to 400° F (200° C)
Preheated baking stone *or* baking sheet, lightly greased

1 1/4 cups	water	300 mL
1 tsp	salt	5 mL
3 tbsp	granulated sugar	45 mL
3 3/4 cups	all-purpose flour or bread flour	925 mL
4	medium cloves garlic, roasted	4
2 tsp	bread machine yeast	10 mL

You'll love these mild, sweet garlic bagels. Roasting mellows the garlic flavor.

TIP

When roasting garlic, be sure you don't use too much oil.

VARIATION

Substitute 2 to 3 cloves minced fresh garlic (no more!) for the roasted.

1. Measure ingredients into baking pan in the order recommended by the manufacturer. Place pan in the oven chamber. Select **Dough Cycle**.

2. Remove dough to a lightly floured surface; cover with a large bowl and let rest for 10 to 15 minutes. Shape the dough into a round cylinder 12 inches (30 cm) long. Cut into 8 portions 1 1/2 inches (4 cm) wide. Push thumbs through the center of each piece and pull into a bagel shape, rounding all the surfaces.

3. Place dough on prepared baking sheet; cover and let rise in a warm, draft-free place for 30 to 45 minutes or until doubled in volume.

4. Bring a large pot of water and 1 tbsp (15 mL) sugar to a gentle yet full boil. Immerse bagels in water one at a time, turning upside down. Hold under the water for 20 seconds with a skimmer or large spoon until the dough becomes a little puffy.

5. Bake on the preheated baking stone or prepared baking sheet in preheated oven for 15 minutes or until the bagels sound hollow when tapped on the bottom.

Sun-Dried Tomato Basil Bagels

MAKES **8** BAGELS		

Preheat oven to 400° F (200° C)
Preheated baking stone *or* baking sheet, lightly greased

1 cup	tomato vegetable juice	250 mL
2 tbsp	granulated sugar	25 mL
2 1/2 cups	all-purpose flour or bread flour	625 mL
1/3 cup	snipped sun-dried tomatoes	75 mL
2 tsp	dried basil	10 mL
2 tsp	bread machine yeast	10 mL

1. Measure ingredients into baking pan in the order recommended by the manufacturer. Place pan in the oven chamber. Select **Dough Cycle**.

2. Remove dough to a lightly floured surface; cover with a large bowl and let rest for 10 to 15 minutes. Shape the dough into a round cylinder 12 inches (30 cm) long. Cut into 8 portions 1 1/2 inches (4 cm) wide. Push thumbs through the center of each piece and pull into a bagel shape, rounding all the surfaces.

3. Place dough on prepared baking sheet; cover and let rise in a warm, draft-free place for 30 to 45 minutes or until doubled in volume.

4. Bring a large pot of water and 1 tbsp (15 mL) sugar to a gentle yet full boil. Immerse bagels in water one at a time, turning upside down. Hold under the water for 20 seconds with a skimmer or large spoon until the dough becomes a little puffy.

5. Bake on the preheated baking stone or prepared baking sheet in preheated oven for 15 minutes or until the bagels sound hollow when tapped on the bottom.

The star attraction of a special luncheon, add smoked turkey, crisp lettuce, a juicy tomato slice and freshly grated Parmesan cheese to this brightly colored, flavorful bagel.

TIP

Snip soft sun-dried tomatoes into large 1/2-inch (1 cm) pieces for an extra burst of tomato goodness.

VARIATION

Use dried tarragon, thyme or oregano in place of basil.

Whole Wheat Bagels

MAKES 6 TO 8 BAGELS

Preheat oven to 400° F (200° C)
Preheated baking stone *or* baking sheet, lightly greased

1 1/4 cups	water	300 mL
1 tsp	salt	5 mL
1/4 cup	packed brown sugar	50 mL
2 1/2 cups	whole wheat flour	625 mL
2 tsp	bread machine yeast	10 mL

1. Measure ingredients into baking pan in the order recommended by the manufacturer. Place pan in the oven chamber. Select **Dough Cycle**.

2. Remove dough to a lightly floured surface; cover with a large bowl and let rest for 10 to 15 minutes. Shape the dough into a round cylinder 12 inches (30 cm) long. Cut into 8 portions 1 1/2 inches (4 cm) wide. Push thumbs through the center of each piece and pull into a bagel shape, rounding all the surfaces.

3. Place dough on prepared baking sheet; cover and let rise in a warm, draft-free place for 30 to 45 minutes or until doubled in volume.

4. Bring a large pot of water and 1 tbsp (15 mL) sugar to a gentle yet full boil. Immerse bagels in water one at a time, turning upside down. Hold under the water for 20 seconds with a skimmer or large spoon until the dough becomes a little puffy.

5. Bake on the preheated baking stone or prepared baking sheet in preheated oven for 15 minutes or until the bagels sound hollow when tapped on the bottom.

A whole-grain bread flavor and texture make this a real treat for all bagel lovers.

TIP

Stone-ground whole wheat flour is a coarser grind that makes the texture of the bagel slightly heavier.

VARIATION

Bagel chips are great snacks. Cut bagels in half and slice 1/8 inch (2 mm) thick. Brush with olive oil and bake at 400° F (200° C) for 12 minutes or until crisp.

ROLLS BY THE BASKETFUL

*Here are the recipes that will have your bread baskets brimming
with a magical assortment of rolls. The shapes vary from perfectly round globes to triangular-shaped wedges to narrow sticks.
Sizes range from dainty to enormous, satisfying every appetite.
Bake and freeze an assortment to enjoy later.*

TIPS FOR FORMING, FINISHING AND BAKING ROLLS

1. Forming

Cover dough with a large bowl and allow to rest for 10 to 15 minutes before forming. This allows the gluten in the warm dough to relax, making the dough less sticky and easier to handle.

Handle the dough as little as possible for more tender rolls. Too much flour added to a slightly sticky dough results in tough, heavy, dense rolls.

2. Choosing the shape

Choose any shape you like — whether from those given in the recipe or those described at the end of the chapter. For example, **ALPINE MUESLI ROLLS** (see recipe, page 83) can become Muesli "flower pots" using the technique described for **PUMPERNICKEL FLOWER POTS** (see recipe, page 91). The possible variations are endless. Follow the recipe directions carefully for size and thickness so that your bread will look as appetizing as it tastes.

3. Finishing

Lightly grease the tops of the dough with a cooking spray or shortening. Choose any finish listed under any recipe or at the end of the chapter. Brush the finish on gently so the dough does not deflate.

4. Proofing

Cover the dough with waxed paper and a lint-free towel to keep it warm and protected from drafts as it rises. To test for readiness, press two fingers into the dough; the indentations should remain.

5. Baking

To ensure even browning when baking two pans at the same time, switch their position in the oven halfway through cooking time.

Alpine Muesli Rolls

MAKES 8 ROLLS		

Preheat oven to 375° F (190° C)

1 1/4 cups	water	300 mL
1/4 cup	skim milk powder	50 mL
1 1/2 tsp	salt	7 mL
2 tbsp	honey	25 mL
1 tbsp	shortening	15 mL
2 3/4 cups	all-purpose flour or bread flour	675 mL
1 cup	muesli	250 mL
1 1/2 tsp	bread machine yeast	7 mL
1/4 cup	raisins	50 mL
1/4 cup	raw unsalted sunflower seeds	50 mL

1. Measure all ingredients *except raisins and sunflower seeds* into baking pan in the order recommended by the manufacturer. Insert pan into the oven chamber. Select **Dough Cycle**.

2. Add raisins and sunflower seeds at the "add ingredient" signal or gently knead into dough at end of cycle.

3. Remove dough to a lightly floured surface; cover with a large bowl and allow to rest for 10 to 15 minutes.

4. Choose the shaping and finishing method as given below or from any roll recipe in this chapter.

TOASTIES

Roll out dough to a 12-inch (30 cm) circle. Place on a lightly greased 12-inch (30 cm) pizza pan. Using a pizza wheel, cut into 8 wedges. Cover and let rise in a warm, draft-free place for 30 to 45 minutes or until doubled in volume. Bake at 375° F (190° C) for 25 to 30 minutes or until toasties sound hollow when tapped on the bottom. Cool completely. Slice each triangle in half crosswise and fill with your favorite deli meats.

SEEDS AND MORE SEEDS

Gently brush the risen dough with melted butter or milk. Sprinkle with muesli.

With 8 different nuts and grains — providing tastes ranging from salty to sweet — every bite is a treat.

TIP

Muesli can be purchased at bulk food stores. It becomes rancid quickly so keep in the refrigerator and check for freshness before adding to the baking pan.

Pre-packaged boxed Muesli cereals contain extra fat and sugar and may result in a completely different roll. Choose lower-fat unsweetened products.

VARIATION

Form dough into 4 mini loaves, bake and slice thinly. They're ideal bases for hors d'oeuvres.

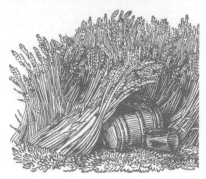

Crunchy Seed Mini-Loaves

Preheat oven to 375° F (190° C)

1 1/4 cups	water	300 mL
1/4 cup	skim milk powder	50 mL
1 1/4 tsp	salt	6 mL
2 tbsp	honey	25 mL
2 tbsp	shortening	25 mL
1 cup	whole wheat flour	250 mL
2 1/4 cups	all-purpose flour or bread flour	550 mL
1/4 cup	pumpkin seeds	50 mL
1/4 cup	sesame seeds	50 mL
1/4 cup	raw unsalted sunflower seeds	50 mL
1 1/2 tsp	bread machine yeast	7 mL

Finish these rolls with seeded toppings for added crunch using a mixture of flax, sunflower, sesame, poppy and pumpkin seeds.

TIP

Brush risen dough lightly with a mixture of 1 egg white and 1 tbsp (15 mL) water to ensure that the seeds will stick.

VARIATION

Vary the proportions of seeds used, but keep the total amount the same as called for in the recipe.

1. Measure ingredients into baking pan in the order recommended by the manufacturer. Insert pan into the oven chamber. Select **Dough Cycle**.

2. Remove dough to a lightly floured surface; cover with a large bowl and allow to rest for 10 to 15 minutes.

3. Choose the shaping and finishing method as described below, or from any roll recipe in this chapter.

MINI-LOAVES

Divide the dough into 8 portions. Form into small loaves. Place in lightly greased mini-loaf pans. Cover and let rise in a warm, draft-free place for 30 to 45 minutes or until doubled in volume. Finish as desired. Bake at 375° F (190° C) for 20 to 25 minutes or until rolls sound hollow when tapped on the bottom.

EXTRA CRUNCH

Gently brush the risen dough with water. Sprinkle sesame, pumpkin or sunflower seeds on the top of the loaves just before baking. The seeds will toast to a crunchy texture.

Crusty French Onion Mini-Sticks

MAKES **12** MINI-STICKS		
Preheat oven to 400° F (200° C)		
1 1/4 cups	water	300 mL
1 1/4 tsp	salt	6 mL
2 tsp	granulated sugar	10 mL
3 1/2 cups	all-purpose flour or bread flour	875 mL
1/2 cup	minced dried onion	125 mL
1 1/4 tsp	bread machine yeast	7 mL

Tear apart these savory mini-sticks and enjoy the flaky crust.

TIP

Dried onion flakes are more convenient than fresh and give a stronger flavor.

Fresh onions are not recommended here since they contain too much water.

Don't add onion salt to enhance the onion flavor.

VARIATION

Cut mini-sticks into thick slices or large cubes and use to top French onion soup.

1. Measure ingredients into baking pan in the order recommended by the manufacturer. Insert pan into the oven chamber. Select **Dough Cycle**.
2. Remove dough to a lightly floured surface; cover with a large bowl and allow to rest for 10 to 15 minutes.
3. Choose the shaping and finishing method as described below or from any roll recipe in this chapter.

MINI FRENCH STICKS

Divide the dough into 12 portions. Form into small loaves, tapering the ends slightly. Place at least 2 inches (5 cm) apart on a baking sheet sprinkled with 2 tbsp (25 mL) cornmeal. Cover and let rise in a warm, draft-free place for 30 to 45 minutes or until doubled in volume. Bake at 400° F (200° C) for 15 to 20 minutes or until the mini-sticks sound hollow when tapped on the bottom.

CRISP AND FLAKY

Place a metal pan containing 12 ice cubes on the bottom rack of the oven. Before baking, let cubes melt. Brush risen dough with cold water. Spritz with cold water every 5 minutes during baking.

Double Cheese Dill Rolls with Dijon Mustard Glaze

What a flavor combination — cheese, dill and a honey mustard glaze!

TIP

Use fresh dill when available.

VARIATION

Try the glaze used here on any cheese bread, rye hearth bread or rolls.

MAKES 18 ROLLS		
Preheat oven to 375° F (190° C)		
1 1/4 cups	water	300 mL
1 tsp	salt	5 mL
1 tbsp	granulated sugar	15 mL
3 1/4 cups	all-purpose or bread flour	800 mL
1/3 cup	buttermilk powder	75 mL
3/4 cup	grated old Cheddar cheese	175 mL
2 tbsp	grated Parmesan cheese	25 mL
1/2 tsp	dill seeds	2 mL
1 tsp	bread machine yeast	5 mL

1. Measure ingredients into baking pan in the order recommended by the manufacturer. Insert pan into the oven chamber. Select **Dough Cycle**.
2. Remove the dough to a lightly floured surface; cover with a large bowl and let rest for 10 to 15 minutes.
3. Choose the shaping and finishing method as described below, or from any roll recipe in this chapter.

FAN TANS

Divide the dough into 3 portions. Roll out each into a 9-inch (23 cm) square. Brush with 1 tbsp (15 mL) melted butter. With a sharp knife, cut each square into 6 strips. Make 3 stacks of 6 strips each. Cut each stack into six 1 1/2-inch (4 cm) pieces. Place fan tans cut-side up, into 18 lightly greased muffin tin cups. Cover and let rise in a warm, draft-free place for 30 to 45 minutes or until doubled in volume. Finish as desired. Bake at 375° F (190° C) for 15 to 20 minutes or until rolls sound hollow when tapped on the bottom.

DIJON MUSTARD GLAZE

Combine 1 egg and 1 tbsp (15 mL) Dijon mustard. Lightly brush over the risen rolls just before baking.

Hamburger and Hot Dog Buns

MAKES **9** TO **12** BUNS		

Preheat oven to 375° F (190° C)

1 1/4 cups	water	300 mL
1	egg	1
1 1/4 tsp	salt	6 mL
2 tbsp	granulated sugar	25 mL
2 tbsp	shortening	25 mL
1 1/2 cups	whole wheat flour	375 mL
2 1/2 cups	all-purpose flour or bread flour	625 mL
1/3 cup	buttermilk powder	75 mL
1 1/4 tsp	bread machine yeast	6 mL

These versatile buns can be made as large or small as your family likes.

VARIATION

Here's a personal favorite: Prepare CHEDDAR BEER BREAD (see recipe, page 12) using the Dough Cycle and finish as hamburger and hot dog buns.

1. Measure ingredients into baking pan in the order recommended by the manufacturer. Insert pan into the oven chamber. Select **Dough Cycle**.
2. Remove dough to a lightly floured surface; cover with a large bowl and let rest for 10 to 15 minutes.
3. Choose from the shaping and finishing methods described below or from any roll recipe in this chapter.

HOT DOG BUNS

Divide the dough into 12 equal portions. Form into 5-inch (12.5 cm) hot-dog-shaped buns. Place the buns on a lightly greased baking sheet. Cover and let rise in a warm, draft-free place for 30 to 45 minutes or until doubled in volume. Bake at 375° F (190° C) for 15 to 18 minutes or until buns sound hollow when tapped on the bottom.

HAMBURGER BUNS

Divide the dough into 9 to 12 portions. Roll each into a ball. Form into a flattened hamburger-bun shape between 3 to 3 1/2 inches (7.5 to 9 cm) in diameter. Place buns on a lightly greased baking sheet. Cover and let rise in a warm, draft-free place for 30 to 45 minutes or until doubled in volume. Bake at 375° F (190° C) for 15 to 20 minutes or until buns sound hollow when tapped on the bottom.

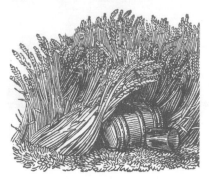

Multigrain Bow Knots

	MAKES **24** BOW KNOTS	

Preheat oven to 375° F (190° C)

1 1/4 cups	water	300 mL
1/4 cup	skim milk powder	50 mL
1 1/2 tsp	salt	7 mL
3 tbsp	granulated sugar	45 mL
2 tbsp	shortening	25 mL
3 cups	all-purpose flour or bread flour	750 mL
1/4 cup	cracked wheat	50 mL
1/4 cup	flax seeds	50 mL
1/4 cup	7-grain cereal	50 mL
2 tbsp	oat bran	25 mL
2 tbsp	wheat germ	25 mL
1 1/2 tsp	bread machine yeast	7 mL

These rolls are a crunchy, nutty treat and go perfectly with a Caesar salad.

TIP

For more uniform ropes, roll pieces of dough on the breadboard — not in the air between your hands.

VARIATION

Make one large free-form bun 10 inches (25 cm) in diameter. Cut in half crosswise, pile on the veggies and cold cuts, and cut into wedges for a nutritious lunch dish.

BOW KNOTS

Divide the dough into 24 equal portions. Roll out each into a 9-inch (23 cm) rope. Tie ropes to make a knot at the center.(Don't pull too tightly.) Place on a lightly greased baking sheet, 2 inches (5 cm) apart. Cover and let rise in a warm, draft-free place for 30 to 45 minutes or until doubled in volume. Finish as desired. Bake at 375° F (190° C) for 15 to 20 minutes or until rolls sound hollow when tapped on the bottom.

1. Measure ingredients into baking pan in the order recommended by the manufacturer. Insert pan into the oven chamber. Select **Dough Cycle**.

2. Remove dough to a lightly floured surface; cover with a large bowl and let rest for 10 to 15 minutes.

3. Choose the shaping and finishing method described at left, or from any roll recipe in this chapter.

Shiny Egg Yolk Glaze

1	egg yolk	1
1 tbsp	water	15 mL
1 tbsp	sesame seeds	15 mL

1. Combine egg yolk and water. Lightly brush over rolls before baking. Sprinkle with sesame seeds.

Mustard Rye Mini-Submarines

MAKES **8** MINI-SUBMARINES		

Preheat oven to 375° F (190° C)

1 1/4 cups	water	300 mL
2 tbsp	prepared mustard	25 mL
1/2 tsp	salt	2 mL
1 tbsp	packed brown sugar	15 mL
2 tbsp	olive oil	25 mL
3/4 cup	whole wheat flour	175 mL
2 cups	all-purpose flour or bread flour	500 mL
3/4 cup	rye flour	175 mL
1 1/4 tsp	bread machine yeast	6 mL

These submarine-shaped rolls are delicious split in half and piled high with Black Forest ham and Swiss cheese or served with bratwurst sausage.

TIP

Add 1/2 tsp (2 mL) mustard seeds to enhance the flavor.

VARIATION

For a slightly milder flavor and lighter colors, substitute light rye flour.

1. Measure ingredients into baking pan in the order recommended by the manufacturer. Insert pan into the oven chamber. Select **Dough Cycle**.
2. Remove dough to a lightly floured surface; cover with a large bowl and let rest for 10 to 15 minutes.
3. Choose the shaping and finishing method described below, or from any roll recipe in this chapter.

MINI SUBMARINE BUNS

Divide the dough into 8 portions. Form into 8 submarine-shaped buns, 4 inches (10 cm) long. Place on a lightly greased baking sheet. Cover and let rise in a warm, draft-free place for 30 to 45 minutes or until doubled in volume. Finish as desired. Bake at 375° F (190° C) for 15 to 20 minutes or until mini-submarines sound hollow when tapped on the bottom.

CENTER SLASHED TOPS

Gently cut one long, deep slash, 1/2 inch (1 cm) lengthwise down the center of the risen roll.

Giant Parmesan-Rosemary Breadsticks

As tasty as they are fun to make, these thin, crunchy sticks are as long as your baking sheet.

TIP

Stretch the ends of the bread sticks as you place them on the baking sheet.

VARIATION

For a spicy treat, add 1 tbsp (15 mL) cracked black peppercorns.

Make these breadsticks in the shape of a focaccia (see recipe, page 52); brush with olive oil and coarse salt.

	MAKES **12** BREADSTICKS	

Preheat oven to 400° F (200° C)

1 1/2 cups	water	375 mL
1/4 cup	skim milk powder	50 mL
1 1/2 tsp	salt	7 mL
1 tbsp	granulated sugar	15 mL
1 tbsp	olive oil	15 mL
3 3/4 cups	all-purpose flour or bread flour	925 mL
1 1/4 tsp	bread machine yeast	6 mL

1. Measure ingredients into baking pan in the order recommended by the manufacturer. Insert pan into the oven chamber. Select **Dough Cycle**.
2. Remove dough to a lightly floured surface; cover with a large bowl and let rest for 10 to 15 minutes.
3. Use the shaping and finishing method described below, or choose from any roll recipe in this chapter.

Parmesan-Rosemary Topping

1 tbsp	minced garlic	15 mL
1 tbsp	olive oil	15 mL
2 tbsp	grated Parmesan cheese	25 mL
2 tsp	dried rosemary	10 mL

1. Brush with a mixture of garlic and olive oil. Sprinkle with Parmesan cheese and rosemary.

GIANT BREADSTICKS

Roll out the dough into a 16- by 6-inch (40 by 15 cm) rectangle. Finish with topping. Cut into 12 strips, 16 inches (40 cm) long and 1/2 inch (1 cm) wide. If shorter breadsticks are preferred, cut into 32 strips, 6 inches (15 cm) long and 1/2 inch (1 cm) wide. Finish with topping. Bake on a lightly greased baking sheet at 400° F (200° C) for 15 to 18 minutes or until breadsticks sound hollow when tapped on the bottom.

Pumpernickel Flower Pots

MAKES 3 OR 4 FLOWER POTS		

Preheat oven to 375° F (190° C)

1 1/4 cups	cold coffee	300 mL
2 tbsp	white vinegar	25 mL
1 tsp	salt	5 mL
3 tbsp	molasses	45 mL
3 tbsp	shortening	45 mL
3 1/4 cups	all-purpose flour or bread flour	800 mL
3/4 cup	rye flour	175 mL
2 tbsp	cocoa	25 mL
2 tsp	caraway seeds	10 mL
1 1/2 tsp	bread machine yeast	7 mL

1. Measure ingredients into baking pan in the order recommended by the manufacturer. Insert pan into the oven chamber. Select **Dough Cycle**.
2. Remove dough to a lightly floured surface; cover with a large bowl and let rest for 10 to 15 minutes.
3. Choose the shaping and finishing method described at left, or from any roll recipe in this chapter.

Glossy Finish

1	egg white, slightly beaten	1
1 tbsp	water	15 mL

1. Combine egg white and water with a fork. Lightly brush on the risen dough just before baking.

Puffed up like little ice cream cones, these rolls make an interesting conversation piece.

TIP

Fill the flower pots only half full with dough. They will double in size during rising and will bake to the perfect size.

VARIATION

Add 1/2 cup (125 mL) raisins at the "add ingredient" signal.

FLOWER POTS

Divide the dough into 3 or 4 portions, depending on the flower pot size. (The dough should only fill the pots half way). Shape into a cone. Place into well-greased, glazed baking pots. Cover and let rise in a warm, draft-free place for 30 to 45 minutes or until doubled in volume. Finish as desired. Bake at 375° F (190° C) for 18 to 25 minutes or until flower pots sound hollow when tapped on the bottom.

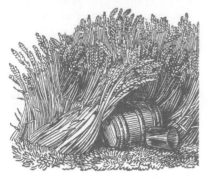

Rich White Dinner Rolls

MAKES 12 ROLLS		

Preheat oven to 375° F (190° C)

1 1/3 cups	milk	325 mL
1 1/4 tsp	salt	6 mL
2 tbsp	granulated sugar	25 mL
2 tbsp	butter	25 mL
3 1/4 cups	all-purpose flour or bread flour	800 mL
1 1/4 tsp	bread machine yeast	6 mL

Delight your family with these cloverleaf rolls. Young children love them when formed into four-leaf clovers.

TIP

For easy removal of baked rolls, spray the inside and bottom of muffin tins with cooking spray.

VARIATION

To make basic pan rolls, divide the dough into 12 portions and place, just touching, in an 8-inch (2 L) pan.

1. Measure ingredients into baking pan in the order recommended by the manufacturer. Insert pan into the oven chamber. Select **Dough Cycle**.

2. Remove dough to a lightly floured surface; cover with a large bowl and let rest for 10 to 15 minutes.

3. Choose the shaping and finishing method described below, or from any roll recipe in this chapter.

CLOVERLEAF ROLLS

Divide the dough into 12 portions. Divide each into 3 pieces. Roll into balls. Place 3 in each cup of a lightly greased muffin tin. Cover and let rise in a warm, draft-free place for 30 to 45 minutes or until doubled in volume. Bake at 375° F (190° C) for 15 to 20 minutes or until rolls sound hollow when tapped on the bottom.

GOLDEN GLAZE

Brush freshly baked rolls with 1 to 2 tbsp (15 to 25 mL) melted butter.

Saffron Currant Bath Buns with Lemon Sugar Glaze

This traditional British favorite originated in the city of Bath. The bun's light, soft texture has the sweet taste of saffron.

TIP

To enhance the flavor of saffron, soak individual strands in boiling water before adding. Allow soaking water to cool to room temperature then use to make up part of the 3/4 cup (175 mL) water called for in the recipe.

Currants discolor the dough when added at the "add ingredient" cycle.

VARIATION

For crispier buns, bake the dough in individual muffin cups.

MAKES 12 BUNS		

Preheat oven to 375° F (190° C)

3/4 cup	water	175 mL
1 tsp	saffron strands	5 mL
2	eggs	2
1 tsp	salt	5 mL
2 tbsp	granulated sugar	25 mL
2 tbsp	butter	25 mL
2 3/4 cups	all-purpose flour or bread flour	675 mL
1/4 cup	buttermilk powder	50 mL
1 tsp	bread machine yeast	5 mL
1 cup	currants	250 mL

1. Measure all ingredients *except currants* into baking pan in the order recommended by the manufacturer. Insert pan into the oven chamber. Select **Dough Cycle**.
2. Remove dough to a lightly floured surface; cover with a large bowl and let rest for 10 to 15 minutes. Knead in currants.
3. Choose the shaping and finishing method for "Round Buns" (see page 96), or from any roll recipe in this chapter.

Lemon Glaze

1 tbsp	lemon juice	15 mL
1	egg white, slightly beaten	1
2 tsp	coarse granulated sugar (optional)	10 mL

1. Brush risen dough with a mixture of lemon juice and egg white. If desired, sprinkle with sugar.

Submarine Buns

Preheat oven to 350° F (180° C)

1 cup	water	250 mL
1	egg	1
1 tsp	salt	5 mL
2 tsp	granulated sugar	10 mL
3 1/3 cups	all-purpose flour or bread flour	825 mL
1 1/2 tsp	bread machine yeast	7 mL

1. Measure ingredients into baking pan in the order recommended by the manufacturer. Insert pan into the oven chamber. Select **Dough Cycle**.
2. Remove dough to a lightly floured surface; cover with a large bowl and let rest for 10 to 15 minutes.
3. Choose the shaping and finishing method given below, or from any roll recipe in this chapter.

SUBMARINE BUNS

Divide the dough into 6 equal portions. Form into slightly flattened 12-inch (30 cm) long buns. Place on a baking sheet sprinkled with cornmeal. Cover and let rise in a warm, draft-free place for 30 to 45 minutes, until doubled in volume. Brush with topping. Bake at 350° F (180° C) for 15 minutes or until buns sound hollow when tapped on the bottom.

Toasted Sesame Seed Topping

1 to 2 tbsp	melted butter	15 to 25 mL
1 to 2 tbsp	sesame seeds	15 to 25 mL

1. Brush the risen dough with butter. Sprinkle with sesame seeds. The seeds will toast as the buns bake.

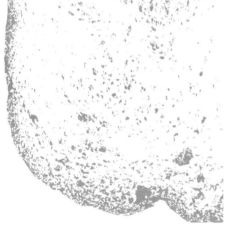

This bun is also known as a hero, hoagie, grinder or, in New Orleans, a muffuletta.

VARIATION

Choose a size to suit individual tastes, making either six 12-inch (30 cm) or twelve 6-inch (15 cm) buns.

Impress your family with Kaisers just like those from the bakeshop. It takes a little practice, but before long you will become an expert.

TIP

Turning the Kaisers upside down to rise and then turning them right-side up just before baking helps to prevent the folds from springing open during baking.

VARIATION

Dust the baking sheet with semolina flour instead of cornmeal.

Whole Wheat Kaisers

MAKES 9 KAISERS		

Preheat oven to 375° F (190° C)

1 1/4 cups	water	300 mL
2	eggs	2
1 1/2 tsp	salt	7 mL
2 tbsp	granulated sugar	25 mL
4 cups	whole wheat flour	1 L
1 1/2 tsp	bread machine yeast	7 mL

1. Measure ingredients into baking pan in the order recommended by the manufacturer. Insert pan into the oven chamber. Select **Dough Cycle**.

2. Remove dough to a lightly floured surface; cover with a large bowl and let rest for 10 to 15 minutes.

3. Choose the shaping and finishing method given below or from any roll recipe in this chapter.

KAISERS

Divide the dough into 9 portions. Roll each into a ball. With a rolling pin, roll out into a 5-inch (12.5 cm) circle. Place the thumb of your left hand at an edge of the circle; fold approximately one-fifth of the circle over your thumb in towards the center. Press firmly into the dough at the center. Repeat four more times, tucking the end of the fifth fold under the first fold in the space left when thumb is removed. Place the buns upside down on a baking sheet. Cover and let rise in a warm, draft-free place for 30 to 45 minutes, or until doubled in volume. Turn right-side up on a baking sheet sprinkled with 1 to 2 tbsp (15 to 25 mL) of cornmeal. Bake at 350° F (180° C) for 15 to 20 minutes or until Kaisers sound hollow when tapped on the bottom.

ADDITIONAL ROLL SHAPES

Prepare any roll recipe from this chapter. Select a shape from below. Proof and bake according to the recipe directions.

BRAIDED WREATHS

Divide any roll dough recipe into 12 equal portions. Divide each portion into thirds. Roll out each piece into a 10-inch (25 cm) rope. Braid the three ropes together, pinching the ends to seal. Place on a lightly greased baking sheet and attach the ends to form a wreath.

CRESCENT ROLLS

Roll out the dough into a rectangle 10 inches (25 cm) wide and 1/8 inch (2 mm) thick. (The length will depend on the amount of dough you are working with.) Cut the dough into triangles with a sharp pizza cutter or knife. Stretch the corners of the long side outward slightly. Roll up the dough to the point. Stretch the point slightly as you roll. Bend into a crescent shape. Be sure the point faces inside and is tucked under so it won't pop up during baking. Any dough recipe can be made into crescents.

OR

Divide the dough in half. Roll each half into a circle 1/8 inch (2 mm) thick (or desired thickness). Cut into 8 to 12 wedges. Follow the shaping instructions described above.

PISTOLET

Divide any roll dough recipe into 18 portions. Form each into a ball. Dust the tops with flour, and press the handle of a wooden spoon into the center of each dough circle to almost split in half. Pull gently to lengthen the roll; the sides will almost come together.

ROUND BUNS

Divide the dough into 12 portions. Roll into balls, flattening slightly. Place on a lightly greased baking sheet, almost touching. Cover and let rise, in a warm, draft-free place for 30 to 45 minutes or until doubled in volume. Bake at 375° F (190° C) for 15 to 20 minutes or until buns sound hollow when tapped on the bottom.

GIANT PARMESAN ROSEMARY BREADSTICKS (PAGE 90) ➤
OVERLEAF: ASSORTMENT OF MONTREAL-STYLE BAGELS (PAGES 72-79)

HEARTH BREADS

Traditionally dough was formed into round loaves and placed on the hearth to rise. The tops were quickly scored, brushed with butter, then baked. The aroma greeted the family as they gathered for meals. You can continue this custom with recipes from this chapter.

◄ SUNNY RYE LOAF (PAGE 109)

TIPS FOR MAKING HEARTH BREADS

1. Forming

Cover with a large bowl, and allow dough to rest for 10 to 15 minutes before forming. If the dough is sticky, flour your hands and add a small amount to the board. Too much flour added at this stage will result in a tough, heavy texture.

Choose any forming method from any hearth bread recipe. Follow the instructions carefully. If the dough keeps shrinking back when rolled, cover and let it rest, for 10 to 15 minutes, then try again. The length of loaves is geared to the common sizes of baking sheets available.

2. Proofing

Cover dough and let rise in a warm, draft-free place until doubled in volume. To test for readiness, press two fingers into the dough; the indents made should remain.

3. Finishing

Choose any finishing method from any hearth bread recipe. Deep cuts, made before or after proofing, will open wider than shallow cuts.

Batarde

MAKES 1 LOAF		

Preheat oven to 425° F (220° C)

1 1/2 cups	water	375 mL
1 1/2 tsp	salt	7 mL
1 tbsp	granulated sugar	15 mL
3 3/4 cups	all-purpose flour or bread flour	950 mL
1 1/2 tsp	bread machine yeast	7 mL

1. Measure ingredients into baking pan in the order recommended by the manufacturer. Insert pan into the oven chamber. Select **Dough Cycle**.
2. Remove dough to a lightly floured surface; cover with a large bowl and let rest for 10 to 15 minutes.
3. Refer to page 98 for instructions on forming, proofing and baking hearth breads.

TRADITIONAL FRENCH

Form dough into a 14-inch (35 cm) stick with a slightly flattened top, tapering at both ends. Place on a baking sheet sprinkled with cornmeal or semolina flour; cover and let rise in a warm, draft-free place for 30 to 45 minutes or until doubled in volume. Finish the loaf as desired. Bake at 425° F (220° C) for 20 to 25 minutes or until loaf sounds hollow when tapped on the bottom.

FRENCH CRUSTY

With a sharp knife, gently cut 5 long parallel diagonal slashes approximately 1/2 inch (1 cm) deep diagonally across the top of the risen loaf. Spritz with cold water just before baking. Repeat frequently during the first 10 minutes of baking.

These long, slender sticks are called pain ordinaire *or "everyday bread" in France. They are served freshly made with every course, from soup to dessert.*

TIP

Crisp with a spritz of water during baking. Bake over a pan of hot water.

VARIATION

Slice leftover loaf into 1-inch (2.5 cm) thick slices to use for French onion soup.

Make mini French loaves. Remember the baked loaf will be double the size of the dough when placed in the pan.

Form into one large round for a *boule*.

Beer Rye Bread

MAKES 1 LOAF		
Preheat oven to 375° F (190° C)		
1 1/4 cups	beer	300 mL
1 1/2 tsp	salt	7 mL
2 tbsp	brown sugar	25 mL
1 tbsp	molasses	15 mL
2 tbsp	shortening	25 mL
3/4 cup	whole wheat flour	200 mL
1 1/2 cups	all-purpose flour or bread flour	375 mL
1 cup	rye flour	250 mL
2 tsp	caraway seeds	10 mL
1 1/4 tsp	bread machine yeast	6 mL

What a combination! The robust flavor of beer complements a dark rye.

TIP

Make this loaf with your choice of either a full-bodied ale or a lighter-flavored lager.

VARIATION

Substituting water for beer will result in a milder, less tangy bread.

1. Measure ingredients into baking pan in the order recommended by the manufacturer. Insert pan into the oven chamber. Select **Dough Cycle**.
2. Remove dough to a lightly floured surface; cover with a large bowl and let rest for 10 to 15 minutes.
3. Refer to page 98 for instructions on forming, proofing and baking hearth breads.

HEARTH

Shape dough into a 9-inch (22.5 cm) round loaf, leaving it higher in the center than at the edges. Place on a lightly greased baking sheet; cover and let rise in a warm, draft-free place for 30 to 45 minutes or until doubled in volume. Finish as desired. Bake at 375° F (190° C) for 35 to 45 minutes or until loaf sounds hollow when tapped on the bottom.

TRIPLE SLASHED

With a sharp knife or a lame, make 3 long parallel slashes 3/4 inch (2 cm) deep from side to side across the top of the risen loaf. These will open during baking, resulting in a football-shaped loaf.

Company Country Grain Bread

Preheat oven to 375° F (190° C)

1 1/4 cups	water	300 mL
1/4 cup	skim milk powder	50 mL
1 1/2 tsp	salt	7 mL
3 tbsp	packed brown sugar	45 mL
2 tbsp	shortening	25 mL
1 cup	whole wheat flour	250 mL
2 cups	all-purpose flour or bread flour	500 mL
1/4 cup	cracked wheat	50 mL
1/4 cup	7-grain cereal	50 mL
2 tbsp	flax seeds	25 mL
2 tbsp	oat bran	25 mL
2 tbsp	wheat germ	25 mL
2 tsp	bread machine yeast	10 mL

This granary-style loaf of wheat, oats and rye is shaped, slashed then baked.

TIP

Slash the top of the dough with a lame just before baking. Deeper slashes produce wider cuts.

VARIATION

Make personal mini-buns 3 inches (7.5 cm) long and 1 inch (2.5 cm) high; taper at the ends and slash lengthwise down the center.

1. Measure ingredients into baking pan in the order recommended by the manufacturer. Insert pan into the oven chamber. Select **Dough Cycle**.
2. Remove dough to a lightly floured surface; cover with a large bowl and let rest for 10 to 15 minutes.
3. Refer to page 98 for instructions on forming, proofing and baking hearth breads.

OVAL

Form the dough into a large oval with a high, rounded top. Place on a lightly greased baking sheet; cover and let rise, covered, in a warm, draft-free place for 30 to 45 minutes or until doubled in volume. Finish as desired. Bake at 375° F (190° C) for 35 to 45 minutes or until loaf sounds hollow when tapped on the bottom.

TRIPLE SLASHED

With a sharp knife, gently cut 3 diagonal slashes 1/2 inch (1 cm) deep on top of the risen loaf.

More crust than bread, this long, flat stick is narrow and tuggy-textured. It should be thickly sliced on the bias.

TIP

To keep the crust nice and crisp, store the loaf loosely covered in a paper bag.

VARIATION

For a crispier crust, place a pan of hot water on the bottom rack of the oven during preheating and spritz with water every 3 to 5 minutes during baking.

Country French Stick

MAKES 1 LOAF		

Preheat oven to 375° F (190° C)

1 1/3 cups	water	325 mL
1 1/2 tsp	salt	7 mL
1 tbsp	granulated sugar	15 mL
3 1/2 cups	all-purpose flour or bread flour	875 mL
1 1/4 tsp	bread machine yeast	6 mL

1. Measure ingredients into baking pan in the order recommended by the manufacturer. Insert pan into the oven chamber. Select **Dough Cycle**.
2. Remove dough to a lightly floured surface; cover with a large bowl and let rest for 10 to 15 minutes.
3. Refer to page 98 for instructions on forming, proofing and baking hearth breads.

FRENCH STICK

Form the dough into a long, thin stick, 14 inches (35 cm) long. Place on a baking sheet sprinkled with cornmeal; cover and let rise in a warm, draft-free place for 30 to 45 minutes or until doubled in volume. Finish as desired. Bake at 375° F (190° C) for 20 to 25 minutes or until loaf sounds hollow when tapped on the bottom.

CHEWY AND CRUSTY

Place a metal pan containing 12 ice cubes on the bottom rack of the oven. Let melt before baking dough. Spritz loaves with water just before baking.

Crusty Italian Bread

MAKES 2 LOAVES		
Preheat oven to 375° F (190° C)		
1 1/3 cups	water	325 mL
1 1/2 tsp	salt	7 mL
1 tbsp	granulated sugar	15 mL
1 tbsp	shortening	15 mL
3 1/3 cups	all-purpose flour or bread flour	825 mL
1 1/4 tsp	bread machine yeast	6 mL

1. Measure ingredients into baking pan in the order recommended by the manufacturer. Insert pan into the oven chamber. Select **Dough Cycle**.

2. Remove dough to a lightly floured surface; cover with a large bowl and let rest for 10 to 15 minutes.

3. Refer to page 98 for instructions on forming, proofing and baking hearth breads.

VIVA ITALIAN

Divide the dough in half. Form each half into a loaf measuring 10 by 4 by 2 inches (25 by 10 by 5 cm) with a slightly flattened top. Place on a baking sheet dusted with cornmeal; cover and let rise in a warm, draft-free place for 30 to 45 minutes or until doubled in volume. Bake at 400° F (200° C) for 20 to 25 minutes or until loaves sound hollow when tapped on the bottom.

SLASH AND DUST

With a sharp knife, gently cut 3 diagonal slashes 1/2 inch (1 cm) deep on top of the risen dough. Dust with flour as soon as it is baked. Do not use with any other wash or glaze.

The perfect bread to serve with cioppino, *a delicious fisherman's stew.*

TIP

Make 3 parallel cuts 1/4 inch (5 mm) deep across the top of the loaf just before baking.

VARIATION

To turn into a crunchy *grissini* (Italian breadstick), form into 18-inch (45 cm) long, thin ropes and bake at 375° F (190° C) for 15 minutes.

New-Fashioned Oatmeal Loaf

MAKES 1 LOAF		
Preheat oven to 375° F (190° C)		
1 1/3 cups	milk	325 mL
1 1/4 tsp	salt	6 mL
3 tbsp	packed brown sugar	45 mL
2 tbsp	shortening	25 mL
1 cup	whole wheat flour	250 mL
2 cups	all-purpose flour or bread flour	500 mL
1/2 cup	quick-cooking oats	125 mL
1/4 cup	oat bran	50 mL
1 1/2 tsp	bread machine yeast	7 mL

Here's an oatmeal loaf updated for the new millennium with oat bran.

TIP

Use small-or medium-flake oatmeal but not the "instant cooking" variety.

VARIATION

Toasting the oats will give a nuttier flavor. Spread in a shallow pan. Bake at 350° F (180° C), stirring frequently, for 10 to 15 minutes or until brown.

1. Measure ingredients into baking pan in the order recommended by the manufacturer. Insert pan into the oven chamber. Select **Dough Cycle**.

2. Remove dough to a lightly floured surface; cover with a large bowl and let rest for 10 to 15 minutes.

3. Refer to page 98 for instructions on forming, proofing and baking hearth breads.

FREE-FORMED HEARTH

Form the dough into a loaf 10 by 3 inches (25 by 7.5 cm) with a slightly flattened top. Place on a lightly greased baking sheet; cover and let rise in a warm, draft-free place for 30 to 45 minutes or until doubled in volume. Bake at 375° F (190° C) for 35 to 40 minutes or until loaf sounds hollow when tapped on the bottom.

THE GRANARY TOUCH

Gently brush the risen loaf with either milk or water. Sprinkle large-flake oatmeal on the top of the loaf just before baking. It will toast to a nutty sweetness.

Pepperoni Wheat Stick

MAKES 1 LOAF		

Preheat oven to 375° F (190° C)

1 1/3 cups	water	325 mL
3/4 tsp	salt	4 mL
2 tsp	granulated sugar	10 mL
1 cup	whole wheat flour	250 mL
2 1/2 cups	all-purpose flour or bread flour	625 mL
2/3 cup	diced pepperoni	150 mL
1/4 cup	snipped fresh parsley	50 mL
1 tsp	cracked peppercorns	5 mL
1 1/2 tsp	bread machine yeast	7 mL

HONEY MUSTARD GLAZE		
1 tbsp	honey	15 mL
1 tbsp	mustard	15 mL

1. Measure ingredients into baking pan in the order recommended by the manufacturer. Insert pan into the oven chamber. Select **Dough Cycle**.
2. Remove dough to a lightly floured surface; cover with a large bowl and let rest for 10 to 15 minutes.
3. Refer to page 98 for instructions on forming, proofing and baking hearth breads.
4. In a bowl mix together honey and mustard; brush on top of baked loaf.

A BIG STICK

Form the dough into a 14- by 3-inch (35 by 7.5 cm) log. Flatten the top slightly and gently taper the ends. Place on a lightly greased baking sheet; cover and let rise in a warm, draft-free place for 30 to 45 minutes or until doubled in volume. Bake at 375° F (190° C) for 20 to 30 minutes or until stick sounds hollow when tapped on the bottom. Apply honey mustard glaze as soon as the stick is baked.

Chunks of salty pepperoni dot this loaf for a taste treat in every bite.

TIP

This large loaf can be baked on a preheated baking stone placed on the bottom rack of the oven.

VARIATION

Substitute Black Forest ham, prosciutto, or any spicy or smoked meat for the pepperoni.

Prairie Bread

MAKES 4 LOAVES		
Preheat oven to 375° F (190° C)		
1 1/3 cups	water	325 mL
1/4 cup	skim milk powder	50 mL
1 tsp	salt	5 mL
1/3 cup	packed brown sugar	75 mL
3 tbsp	vegetable oil	45 mL
1 1/4 cups	whole wheat flour	300 mL
2 cups	all-purpose flour or bread flour	500 mL
3/4 cup	rye flour	175 mL
1 3/4 tsp	bread machine yeast	8 mL

Here's a favorite recipe that combines 3 popular bread flours.

TIP

To make a traditional loaf with puréed raisins, soak large Muscat raisins in water for a few minutes before preparing this recipe. They will purée during the kneading cycle.

VARIATION

Vary the color of this loaf by choosing different types of rye flour.

1. Measure ingredients into baking pan in the order recommended by the manufacturer. Insert pan into the oven chamber. Select **Dough Cycle**.

2. Remove dough to a lightly floured surface; cover with a large bowl and let rest for 10 to 15 minutes.

3. Refer to page 98 for instructions on forming, proofing and baking hearth breads.

FIT FOR A KING

Divide dough in half. Form each half into two 6-inch (15 cm) round loaves. Place on a lightly greased baking sheet; cover and let rise in a warm, draft-free place for 30 to 45 minutes or until doubled in volume. Score top to form the crown. Bake at 375° F (190° C) for 20 to 25 minutes or until loaves sound hollow when tapped on the bottom.

EIGHT-POINT CROWN

Cut 4 intersecting slashes, 1/4 inch (5 mm) deep on the top of each loaf. Slashes made before the dough rises will open wider than slashes made on the risen dough. Your choice!

ROUND AND RUSTIC

Form the dough into a large, slightly flattened, rounded loaf. Place on a lightly greased baking sheet; cover and let rise in a warm, draft-free place for 30 to 45 minutes or until doubled in volume. Finish as desired. Bake at 375° F (190° C) for 35 to 45 minutes or until loaf sounds hollow when tapped on the bottom.

Russian Black Bread

MAKES 1 LOAF		
Preheat oven to 375° F (190° C)		
1 1/2 cups	cold coffee	375 mL
3 tbsp	white vinegar	45 mL
1 1/4 tsp	salt	6 mL
1/4 cup	molasses	50 mL
2 tbsp	shortening	25 mL
3 1/2 cups	all-purpose flour or bread flour	875 mL
1 cup	rye flour	250 mL
1/2 cup	buttermilk powder	125 mL
1/4 cup	wheat berries, cooked	50 mL
2 tbsp	cocoa	25 mL
1 tbsp	caraway seeds	15 mL
1 1/2 tsp	bread machine yeast	7 mL

1. Measure ingredients into baking pan in the order recommended by the manufacturer. Insert pan into the oven chamber. Select **Dough Cycle**.
2. Remove dough to a lightly floured surface; cover with a large bowl and let rest for 10 to 15 minutes.
3. Refer to page 98 for instructions on forming, proofing and baking hearth breads.

CHILD'S 'X AND O' BOARD

With a sharp knife, cut 5 parallel slashes 1/4 inch (5 mm) deep both lengthwise and crosswise to form squares on the surface of the risen dough. Dust the freshly baked loaf with flour for an added color contrast.

SPINACH DIP		
10 oz	thawed chopped spinach, well drained	300 g
8 oz	softened cream cheese	250 g
1 cup	yogurt or sour cream	250 mL
1	small chopped onion	1
1	pkg (4 oz [125 g]) vegetable soup mix	1

1. In a bowl combine all dip ingredients until well mixed.

Company coming? Hollow out and fill this round loaf with the ever-popular spinach dip. (See below.)

TIP

Use fancy molasses rather than the blackstrap, variety, which contains extra sulphur (not a good mix with yeast).

To cook wheat berries, cover with water and allow to stand overnight. Simmer for 30 to 45 minutes or until tender. Drain and cool completely.

VARIATION

For a dinner party, make personal-sized loaves for each of your guests.

Combine all dip ingredients at least 2 or 3 hours ahead; refrigerate to allow the flavors to blend. Just before serving, fill the loaf and serve with cubed bread for dipping.

Settler's Cracked Wheat Braid

MAKES 1 BRAID		
1 1/4 cups	water	300 mL
1 1/4 tsp	salt	6 mL
2 tbsp	packed brown sugar	25 mL
2 tbsp	shortening	25 mL
1 1/4 cups	whole wheat flour	300 mL
2 cups	all-purpose flour or bread flour	500 mL
1/2 cup	cracked wheat	125 mL
1/3 cup	buttermilk powder	75 mL
1 1/2 tsp	bread machine yeast	7 mL

Midwesterners like to place this oval loaf on a large wooden board to slice and serve at the table.

TIP

This is another good loaf to bake on a preheated baking stone placed on the bottom rack of the oven.

VARIATION

For added variety in flavor and texture, try substituting one of the many types wheat-blend flours that are available.

1. Measure ingredients into baking pan in the order recommended by the manufacturer. Insert pan into the oven chamber. Select **Dough Cycle**.

2. Remove dough to a lightly floured surface; cover with a large bowl and let rest for 10 to 15 minutes.

3. Refer to page 98 for instructions on forming, proofing and baking hearth breads.

BRAID

Form the dough into three 12-inch (30 cm) ropes of equal diameter. Braid, tucking the ends under the loaf. Place on a lightly greased baking sheet; cover and let rise in a warm, draft-free place for 30 to 45 minutes or until doubled in volume. Finish as desired. Bake at 375° F (190° C) for 40 to 45 minutes or until braid sounds hollow when tapped on the bottom.

SHINY WITH A CRUNCH

Gently brush the risen dough with melted butter or milk. Sprinkle with cracked wheat or bulgur.

Sunny Rye Loaf

MAKES 1 LOAF		
Preheat oven to 375° F (190° C)		
1 1/4 cups	water	300 mL
1/4 cup	skim milk powder	50 mL
1 1/4 tsp	salt	6 mL
1 tbsp	honey	15 mL
1 tbsp	molasses	15 mL
2 tbsp	shortening	25 mL
1 1/4 cups	whole wheat flour	300 mL
1 1/4 cups	all-purpose flour or bread flour	300 mL
1/2 cup	rye flour	125 mL
1/2 cup	raw, unsalted sunflower seeds	125 mL
2 tsp	orange zest	10 mL
1 1/4 tsp	bread machine yeast	6 mL

This wholesome, rustic-looking loaf is crusty outside but moist inside.

TIP

Rye doughs become very sticky if over-kneaded. Handle quickly after dough is placed on the floured board.

Purchase raw, unsalted sunflower seeds. If only roasted sunflower seeds are available, rinse under hot water and dry well before using.

VARIATION

This dough makes great bread sticks.

1. Measure ingredients into baking pan in the order recommended by the manufacturer. Insert pan into the oven chamber. Select **Dough Cycle**.
2. Remove dough to a lightly floured surface; cover with a large bowl and let rest for 10 to 15 minutes.
3. Refer to page 98 for instructions on forming, proofing and baking hearth breads.

LONG OVAL

Form dough into a log measuring 14 by 4 by 2 inches (35 by 10 by 5 cm) with a slightly flattened top. Place on a lightly greased baking sheet; cover and let rise in a warm, draft-free place for 30 to 45 minutes or until doubled in volume. Finish as desired. Bake at 375° F (190° C) for 30 to 35 minutes or until loaf sounds hollow when tapped on the bottom.

CRUNCHY WITH SUNFLOWER SEEDS

Gently brush the risen loaf with melted butter or milk. Sprinkle with sunflower seeds.

Swedish Limpa Mini Hearth

Makes 4 mini hearths

Preheat oven to 375° F (190° C)

1 1/3 cups	water	325 mL
1 1/2 tsp	salt	7 mL
1/4 cup	dark corn syrup	50 mL
2 tbsp	butter	25 mL
1 1/4 cups	whole wheat flour	300 mL
1 1/2 cups	all-purpose flour or bread flour	375 mL
1 cup	rye flour	250 mL
2 tsp	anise seeds	10 mL
2 tsp	caraway seeds	10 mL
2 tsp	fennel seeds	10 mL
2 tsp	orange zest	10 mL
1 1/2 tsp	bread machine yeast	7 mL

The traditional Scandinavian trio of anise, caraway and fennel seeds give this orange-scented rye loaf a unique flavor.

TIP

For a smoother texture, use a food mill to grind the caraway, fennel and anise seeds.

VARIATION

To heighten the orange flavor, add 1/2 tsp (2 mL) orange extract to the liquid.

1. Measure ingredients into baking pan in the order recommended by the manufacturer. Insert pan into the oven chamber. Select **Dough Cycle**.
2. Remove dough to a lightly floured surface; cover with a large bowl and let dough rest for 10 to 15 minutes.
3. Refer to page 98 for instructions on forming, proofing and baking hearth breads.

MINI HEARTHS

Divide dough into 4 portions. Form each into a 2 1/2-inch (6 cm) round loaf, leaving it higher in the center than at the edges. Place on a lightly greased baking sheet; cover and let rise in a warm, draft-free place for 30 to 45 minutes or until doubled in volume. Finish as desired. Bake at 375° F (190° C) for 15 to 20 minutes or until loaves sound hollow when tapped on the bottom.

"X " MARKS THE SPOT

With a sharp knife or a lame, make 2 intersecting cuts 3/4 inch (2 cm) deep from side to side, in the shape of an "X", across the top of the risen loaves. These will open during baking.

GRAINS, SEEDS AND NUTS

High-fiber multigrain breads have become the choice of today's health-conscious baker. Breads made from grains, seeds and nuts in this chapter are excellent choices.

The Fat/Fiber Connection

Canada's "Food Guide to Healthy Living" states that we should eat 5 to 12 servings from the grain products food group each day. It also recommends we choose whole grain and enriched products more often.

Research suggests fiber aids in lowering blood cholesterol levels and modifies the absorption of sugar by the body. Dietary fiber is found in wheat bran, whole grains, beans, oats, fruits and vegetables. Grain products are also an excellent source of fiber, the major B vitamins and iron. Included in this group are cold and hot cereals, pasta, rice, and all types of breads from bagels to hamburger buns, to pitas and loaves of whole grain bread.

Apple Date Granola Bread

1.5 LB (750 G)		
3/4 cup	unsweetened apple juice	175 mL
2/3 cup	unsweetened applesauce	150 mL
1 tsp	salt	5 mL
2 tbsp	honey	25 mL
2 tbsp	shortening	25 mL
1 cup	whole wheat flour	250 mL
2 cups	all-purpose flour or bread flour	500 mL
2/3 cup	whole pitted dates	150 mL
1/3 cup	granola	75 mL
1 tsp	cinnamon	5 mL
1 1/2 tsp	bread machine yeast	7 mL

2 LB (1 KG)		
1 cup	unsweetened apple juice	250 mL
2/3 cup	unsweetened applesauce	150 mL
1 1/4 tsp	salt	6 mL
2 tbsp	honey	25 mL
2 tbsp	shortening	25 mL
1 1/2 cups	whole wheat flour	375 mL
2 cups	all-purpose flour or bread flour	500 mL
3/4 cup	whole pitted dates	175 mL
1/2 cup	granola	125 mL
1 1/4 tsp	cinnamon	6 mL
1 1/2 tsp	bread machine yeast	7 mL

1. Measure ingredients into baking pan in the order recommended by the manufacturer. Insert pan into the oven chamber.
2. Select **Whole Wheat Cycle**.

Naturally sweetened with apple juice and dates, this crunchy granola loaf doesn't need butter.

TIP

The applesauce and apple juice should be at room temperature.

Look for unsweetened granola at your bulk food store. If unavailable, decrease the honey in the recipe by 1 to 2 tsp (5 to 10 mL) depending on the natural level of sweetness of the granola.

VARIATION

For a sweeter, nuttier flavor you can substitute muesli for the granola.

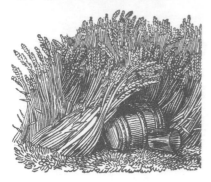

Autumn Pumpkin Seed Bread

A fall celebration of color, texture and flavor, this bread has toasted pumpkin seeds for crunch.

TIP

Canned pumpkin must be at room temperature or the loaf will be short and heavy.

When using fresh pumpkin, ensure that it has the same consistency as canned.

VARIATION

Substitute fresh pumpkin for the canned — but not pumpkin pie filling — also at room temperature.

1.5 LB (750 G)		
1/3 cup	water	75 mL
2/3 cup	canned pumpkin	150 mL
1	egg	1
1/4 cup	skim milk powder	50 mL
1 tsp	salt	5 mL
1/4 cup	packed brown sugar	50 mL
2 tbsp	shortening	25 mL
3/4 cup	whole wheat flour	175 mL
1 3/4 cups	all-purpose flour or bread flour	400 mL
1/3 cup	pumpkin seeds	75 mL
1/2 tsp	ground allspice	2 mL
1/4 tsp	ground ginger	1 mL
1/4 tsp	ground nutmeg	1 mL
1 3/4 tsp	bread machine yeast	8 mL

2 LB (1 KG)		
1/2 cup	water	125 mL
1 cup	canned pumpkin	250 mL
1	egg	1
1/4 cup	skim milk powder	50 mL
1 1/2 tsp	salt	7 mL
1/3 cup	packed brown sugar	75 mL
2 tbsp	shortening	25 mL
1 cup	whole wheat flour	250 mL
2 1/4 cups	all-purpose flour or bread flour	550 mL
1/2 cup	pumpkin seeds	125 mL
3/4 tsp	ground allspice	3 mL
1/2 tsp	ground ginger	2 mL
1/4 tsp	ground nutmeg	1 mL
1 1/2 tsp	bread machine yeast	7 mL

1. Measure ingredients into baking pan in the order recommended by the manufacturer. Insert pan into the oven chamber.
2. Select **Whole Wheat Cycle**.

Applesauce Oatmeal Walnut Bread

Try this heavier-textured bread, which has the sweet taste of apples and the crunch of walnuts.

TIP

Choose unsweetened applesauce for this recipe; the sweetened variety may affect the loaf's appearance.

VARIATION

You can add up to 1/4 cup (50 mL) extra grated apple or chunks of apple without changing the appearance of the loaf.

1.5 LB (750 G)		
1/2 cup	grated apple	125 mL
1/2 cup	unsweetened applesauce	125 mL
1	egg	1
1 1/2 tsp	salt	7 mL
3 tbsp	granulated sugar	45 mL
2 tbsp	shortening	25 mL
1 cup	whole wheat flour	250 mL
1 1/4 cups	all-purpose flour or bread flour	300 mL
1/2 cup	quick-cooking oatmeal	125 mL
1/2 cup	chopped walnuts	125 mL
1 1/2 tsp	bread machine yeast	7 mL

2 LB (1 KG)		L
2/3 cup	grated apple	150 mL
2/3 cup	unsweetened applesauce	150 mL
2	eggs	2
1 1/2 tsp	salt	7 mL
3 tbsp	granulated sugar	45 mL
2 tbsp	shortening	25 mL
1 1/2 cups	whole wheat flour	375 mL
2 cups	all-purpose flour or bread flour	500 mL
3/4 cup	quick-cooking oatmeal	175 mL
3/4 cup	chopped walnuts	175 mL
1 1/2 tsp	bread machine yeast	7 mL

1. Measure ingredients into baking pan in the order recommended by the manufacturer. Insert pan into the oven chamber.
2. Select **Whole Wheat Cycle**.

Country Harvest Bread

1.5 LB (750 G)		
1 1/4 cups	water	300 mL
1/4 cup	skim milk powder	50 mL
1 1/2 tsp	salt	7 mL
2 tbsp	honey	25 mL
2 tbsp	shortening	25 mL
1 cup	whole wheat flour	250 mL
2 cups	all-purpose flour or bread flour	500 mL
1/4 cup	flax seeds	50 mL
2 tbsp	sunflower seeds raw, unsalted	25 mL
1 tbsp	sesame seeds	15 mL
1 3/4 tsp	bread machine yeast	8 mL

2 LB (1 KG)		
1 1/3 cups	water	325 mL
1/4 cup	skim milk powder	50 mL
1 1/2 tsp	salt	7 mL
3 tbsp	honey	45 mL
3 tbsp	shortening	45 mL
1 1/4 cups	whole wheat flour	300 mL
2 1/3 cups	all purpose flour or bread flour	575 mL
1/3 cup	flax seeds	75 mL
1/4 cup	sunflower seeds raw, unsalted	50 mL
2 tbsp	sesame seeds	25 mL
1 3/4 tsp	bread machine yeast	8 mL

1. Measure ingredients into baking pan in the order recommended by the manufacturer. Insert pan into the oven chamber.
2. Select **Whole Wheat Cycle**.

One of our personal favorites, this is a perfect sandwich bread. Smoked turkey, sliced tomatoes and a thin spread of Honey Dijon dressing is all you need.

TIP

To prevent the seeds from becoming rancid, store in an airtight container in the refrigerator.

VARIATION

Try different types of seeds in the recipe, but keep the total amount the same. Choices include pumpkin or poppy seeds.

Chunky Walnut Bread

1.5 LB (750 G)		
1 1/4 cups	water	300 mL
1/4 cup	skim milk powder	50 mL
1 1/4 tsp	salt	6 mL
1 tbsp	packed brown sugar	15 mL
1 tbsp	walnut oil	15 mL
3 cups	all-purpose flour or bread flour	750 mL
3/4 cup	chopped walnuts	175 mL
1 tsp	bread machine yeast	5 mL

2 LB (1 KG)		
1 1/3 cups	water	325 mL
1/4 cup	skim milk powder	50 mL
1 1/2 tsp	salt	7 mL
3 tbsp	packed brown sugar	45 mL
2 tbsp	walnut oil	25 mL
3 1/2 cups	all-purpose flour or bread flour	875 mL
1 cup	chopped walnuts	250 mL
1 1/4 tsp	bread machine yeast	6 mL

The sweetness of the oatmeal in this recipe complements the tang of the walnuts. Serve as an after-school snack with wedges of old Cheddar cheese.

TIP

Taste the walnuts for freshness before adding.

Use olive oil if walnut oil is not available.

VARIATION

Substitute an equal amount of pecans, or shredded unsweetened coconut for the walnuts.

1. Measure ingredients into baking pan in the order recommended by the manufacturer. Insert the pan into the oven chamber.
2. Select **Basic Cycle**.

European Black Bread with Anise Seeds

1.5 LB (750 G)		
1 1/4 cups	water	300 mL
2 tbsp	white vinegar	25 mL
1 tsp	salt	5 mL
1/4 cup	molasses	50 mL
2 tbsp	shortening	25 mL
2 1/3 cups	all-purpose flour or bread flour	575 mL
3/4 cup	rye flour	175 mL
1/3 cup	buttermilk powder	75 mL
1 tbsp	cocoa	15 mL
2 tsp	anise seeds	10 mL
1 tsp	instant coffee granules	5 mL
1 tsp	onion powder	5 mL
1 1/4 tsp	bread machine yeast	6 mL

2 LB (1 KG)		
1 1/2 cups	water	375 mL
3 tbsp	white vinegar	45 mL
1 1/4 tsp	salt	6 mL
1/4 cup	molasses	50 mL
2 tbsp	shortening	25 mL
3 1/2 cups	all-purpose flour or bread flour	875 mL
1 cup	rye flour	250 mL
1/2 cup	buttermilk powder	125 mL
1 tbsp	cocoa	15 mL
1 tbsp	anise seeds	15 mL
2 tsp	instant coffee granules	10 mL
1 1/2 tsp	onion powder	7 mL
1 1/2 tsp	bread machine yeast	7 mL

Adapted from a European recipe, this bread is delicious as an open-faced sandwich with smoked salmon, cream cheese and a hint of dill.

TIP

Use cold leftover coffee to replace the water and instant coffee granules.

Be sure you don't use onion salt for onion powder in bread machine recipes.

VARIATION

Add 2 to 3 tsp (10 to 15 mL) dill, fennel or caraway seeds after the flour.

1. Measure ingredients into baking pan in the order recommended by the manufacturer. Insert pan into the oven chamber.
2. Select **Basic Cycle**.

Five-Seed Rye Bread

1.5 LB (750 G)		
1 1/4 cups	water	300 mL
1/4 cup	skim milk powder	50 mL
1 1/4 tsp	salt	6 mL
2 tbsp	packed brown sugar	25 mL
2 tbsp	shortening	25 mL
3 1/4 cups	all-purpose flour or bread flour	625 mL
1/2 cup	rye flour	125 mL
2 tbsp	flax seeds	25 mL
2 tbsp	poppy seeds	25 mL
2 tbsp	sesame seeds	25 mL
1/2 tsp	caraway seeds	2 mL
1/2 tsp	fennel seeds	2 mL
1 tsp	bread machine yeast	5 mL

2 LB (1 KG)		
1 1/2 cups	water	375 mL
1/4 cup	skim milk powder	50 mL
1 1/2 tsp	salt	7 mL
2 tbsp	packed brown sugar	25 mL
2 tbsp	shortening	25 mL
3 cups	all-purpose flour or bread flour	750 mL
3/4 cup	rye flour	175 mL
1/4 cup	flax seeds	50 mL
1/4 cup	poppy seeds	50 mL
1/4 cup	sesame seeds	50 mL
1 tsp	caraway seeds	5 mL
1 tsp	fennel seeds	5 mL
1 1/2 tsp	bread machine yeast	7 mL

Simmer a crock pot of stew and set the timer for this crunchy loaf. Perfect for inviting the gang back for an "aprés-ski" supper.

TIP

For an attractive topping, sprinkle a mixture of the five seeds over the loaf during the last 10 minutes of baking.

VARIATION

Substitute other seeds for those called for here, making sure the total volume remains the same. Use smaller amounts of stronger-tasting seeds.

1. Measure ingredients into baking pan in the order recommended by the manufacturer. Insert pan into the oven chamber.
2. Select **Basic Cycle**.

Monique's Honey Wheat Bran Bread

1.5 LB (750 G)		
1 cup	water	250 mL
1	egg	1
1/4 cup	skim milk powder	50 mL
1 1/4 tsp	salt	6 mL
1/4 cup	honey	50 mL
2 tbsp	shortening	25 mL
3 1/2 cups	wheat blend flour	875 mL
1 1/2 tsp	bread machine yeast	6 mL

2 LB (1 KG)		L
1 1/3 cups	water	325 mL
1	egg	1
1/4 cup	skim milk powder	50 mL
1 1/2 tsp	salt	7 mL
1/4 cup	honey	50 mL
2 tbsp	shortening	25 mL
4 1/2 cups	wheat blend flour	1.25 L
1 1/2 tsp	bread machine yeast	7 mL

1. Measure ingredients into baking pan in the order recommended by the manufacturer. Insert pan into the oven chamber.
2. Select **Whole Wheat Cycle**.

This high-fiber bread has a delicate taste of honey you will enjoy.

TIP

Be sure you don't increase the bran content (in Variation, below), since it cuts the gluten strands in the flour and the loaf will collapse.

VARIATION

Substitute 1 cup (250 mL) of all-purpose or bread flour, 1/2 cup (125 mL) natural wheat bran and the remaining amount of whole wheat flour for the total amount of wheat blend flour in the recipe.

Oatmeal Molasses Bread

1.5 LB (750 G)		
1 1/4 cups	water	300 mL
1/4 cup	skim milk powder	50 mL
1 1/2 tsp	salt	6 mL
3 tbsp	molasses	40 mL
2 tbsp	shortening	25 mL
1 1/2 cups	whole wheat flour	400 mL
3/4 cup	all-purpose flour or bread flour	200 mL
2/3 cup	quick-cooking oats	150 mL
1/3 cup	7-grain cereal	75 mL
1 1/2 tsp	bread machine yeast	6 mL

2 LB (1 KG)		
1 1/2 cups	water	375 mL
1/4 cup	skim milk powder	50 mL
1 1/2 tsp	salt	7 mL
1/4 cup	molasses	50 mL
2 tbsp	shortening	25 mL
2 cups	whole wheat flour	500 mL
1 1/4 cups	all-purpose flour or bread flour	300 mL
3/4 cup	quick-cooking oats	175 mL
1/2 cup	7-grain cereal	125 mL
1 1/2 tsp	bread machine yeast	7 mL

Oatmeal breads always have a moist, heavy texture. You will enjoy this strong-flavored, slightly tart recipe.

TIP

This loaf frequently has a rough top, since neither the oatmeal nor the grain cereal contain enough cell-building gluten to form a rounded crown.

Use a medium-flaked oatmeal, not an instant, for the best texture in this loaf.

VARIATION

Substitute a 12-grain cereal or muesli for the 7-grain.

1. Measure ingredients into baking pan in the order recommended by the manufacturer. Insert pan into the oven chamber.
2. Select **Whole Wheat Cycle**.

Orange Honey Cracked Wheat Bread

1.5 LB (750 G)		
1 1/3 cups	unsweetened orange juice	325 mL
1/4 cup	skim milk powder	50 mL
1 1/2 tsp	salt	7 mL
1/4 cup	honey	50 mL
2 tbsp	shortening	25 mL
3 1/4 cups	all-purpose flour or bread flour	800 mL
2/3 cup	cracked wheat	150 mL
2 tsp	orange zest	10 mL
1 1/2 tsp	bread machine yeast	7 mL

2 LB (1 KG)		
1 1/2 cups	unsweetened orange juice	375 mL
1/4 cup	skim milk powder	50 mL
1 1/2 tsp	salt	7 mL
1/3 cup	honey	75 mL
3 tbsp	shortening	45 mL
3 3/4 cups	all-purpose flour or bread flour	925 mL
1 cup	cracked wheat	250 mL
1 tbsp	orange zest	15 mL
1 1/2 tsp	bread machine yeast	7 mL

1. Measure ingredients into baking pan in the order recommended by the manufacturer. Insert pan into the oven chamber.
2. Select **Basic Cycle**.

Let the delicious aroma of this freshly baked bread greet you on a lazy Sunday morning. Set the timer instead of the alarm. What a way to wake up!

TIP

Zest the whole orange and freeze any leftovers for the next time you make this loaf. Be careful not to include any of the bitter white part of the orange.

VARIATION

Add 1/2 cup (125 mL) chopped walnuts, pecans or pine nuts. These can be added to the bread pan after the flour. You do not need to wait for the "add ingredient" signal.

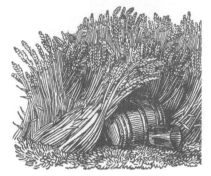

Pilgrims' Multigrain Bread

1.5 LB (750 G)		
1 1/4 cups	water	300 mL
1	egg	1
1 1/2 tsp	salt	7 mL
2 tbsp	packed brown sugar	25 mL
2 tbsp	vegetable oil	25 mL
3 cups	all-purpose flour or bread flour	750 mL
1/3 cup	buttermilk powder	75 mL
1/4 cup	quick-cooking oats	50 mL
1/4 cup	wheat bran	50 mL
2 tbsp	wheat germ	25 mL
1 1/2 tsp	bread machine yeast	7 mL

2 LB (1 KG)		L
1 1/3 cups	water	325 mL
2	eggs	2
1 1/2 tsp	salt	7 mL
3 tbsp	packed brown sugar	45 mL
2 tbsp	vegetable oil	25 mL
3 1/2 cups	all-purpose flour or bread flour	875 mL
1/2 cup	buttermilk powder	125 mL
1/3 cup	quick-cooking oats	75 mL
1/3 cup	wheat bran	75 mL
3 tbsp	wheat germ	45 mL
1 1/2 tsp	bread machine yeast	7 mL

This honey-sweetened loaf, a blend of seeds and whole grains, is a delicious way to get plenty of fiber.

TIP

Store wheat germ in the refrigerator since it becomes rancid quickly. Taste before adding.

VARIATION

Substitute an equal amount of oat bran for the wheat bran. It will result in a slightly sweeter loaf.

1. Measure ingredients into baking pan in the order recommended by the manufacturer. Insert pan into the oven chamber.
2. Select **Basic Cycle**.

Scandinavian Rye Bread

1.5 LB (750 G)		
1 1/4 cups	beer	300 mL
1	egg	1
3/4 tsp	salt	4 mL
1 tbsp	molasses	15 mL
2 tbsp	packed brown sugar	25 mL
1 tbsp	shortening	15 mL
1 3/4 cups	all-purpose flour or bread flour	450 mL
1 cup	rye flour	250 mL
1 tsp	orange zest	5 mL
1/2 tsp	anise seeds	2 mL
1/2 tsp	caraway seeds	2 mL
1/2 tsp	fennel seeds	2 mL
1 1/2 tsp	bread machine yeast	7 mL

2 LB (1 KG)		
1 1/3 cups	beer	325 mL
2	eggs	2
1 1/2 tsp	salt	7 mL
2 tbsp	molasses	25 mL
2 tbsp	packed brown sugar	25 mL
2 tbsp	shortening	25 mL
2 1/4 cups	all-purpose flour or bread flour	550 mL
1 1/2 cups	rye flour	375 mL
2 tsp	orange zest	10 mL
1 tsp	anise seeds	5 mL
1 tsp	caraway seeds	5 mL
1 tsp	fennel seeds	5 mL
1 3/4 tsp	bread machine yeast	8 mL

The traditional trio of caraway, fennel and anise imparts a distinctive yet subtle flavor to this rye loaf.

TIP

Choose a dark rye flour for a darker colored loaf.

VARIATION

Use a food mill to grind the seasonings — in the Scandinavian style — for a smoother flavor and texture.

1. Measure ingredients into baking pan in the order recommended by the manufacturer. Insert pan into the oven chamber.
2. Select **Basic Cycle**.

Seven-Grain Bran Bread

1.5 LB (750 G)		
1 1/4 cups	water	300 mL
1/4 cup	skim milk powder	50 mL
1 1/4 tsp	salt	6 mL
1 tbsp	honey	15 mL
1 tbsp	molasses	15 mL
2 tbsp	shortening	25 mL
3/4 cup	whole wheat flour	175 mL
2 cups	all-purpose flour or bread flour	500 mL
1/3 cup	bran cereal	75 mL
1/3 cup	7-grain cereal	75 mL
1 tsp	bread machine yeast	5 mL

2 LB (1 KG)		
1 1/2 cups	water	375 mL
1/4 cup	skim milk powder	50 mL
1 1/2 tsp	salt	7 mL
2 tbsp	honey	25 mL
2 tbsp	molasses	25 mL
3 tbsp	shortening	45 mL
1 cup	whole wheat flour	250 mL
2 1/4 cups	all-purpose flour or bread flour	550 mL
1/2 cup	bran cereal	125 mL
1/2 cup	7-grain cereal	125 mL
1 1/4 tsp	bread machine yeast	6 mL

This delicious bread is good for you — but don't tell anybody!

TIP

Choose any low-fat wheat bran cereal sold at the supermarket.

VARIATION

Substitute a 3-grain, 12-grain or multi-grain cereal for the 7-grain variety, keeping the total volume the same.

1. Measure ingredients into baking pan in the order recommended by the manufacturer. Insert pan into the oven chamber.
2. Select **Whole Wheat Cycle**.

Southern Cornmeal Bread

1.5 LB (750 G)		
1 cup	water	250 mL
1	egg	1
1/4 cup	skim milk powder	50 mL
1 1/2 tsp	salt	7 mL
2 tbsp	honey	25 mL
2 tbsp	shortening	25 mL
2 1/2 cups	all-purpose flour or bread flour	625 mL
1/2 cup	cornmeal	125 mL
1 tsp	bread machine yeast	5 mL

2 LB (1 KG)		L
1 1/4 cups	water	300 mL
2	eggs	2
1/4 cup	skim milk powder	50 mL
1 1/2 tsp	salt	7 mL
3 tbsp	honey	45 mL
2 tbsp	shortening	25 mL
3 cups	all-purpose flour or bread flour	750 mL
3/4 cup	cornmeal	175 mL
1 tsp	bread machine yeast	5 mL

Golden in color, soft in texture with a hint of corn, this is the perfect bread to accompany a huge pot of spicy chili.

TIP

For a lighter loaf, place the cornmeal on top of the flour; be sure it doesn't touch the water.

VARIATION

Choose a coarser grind of cornmeal with a deep yellow color for an attractive contrast to dark rye bread in a bread basket.

1. Measure ingredients into baking pan in the order recommended by the manufacturer. Insert pan into the oven chamber.
2. Select **Sweet Cycle**.

Sweet Potato Pecan Bread

1.5 LB (750 G)		
2/3 cup	water	150 mL
1/2 cup	mashed sweet potato	125 mL
1/2 cup	chopped apple	125 mL
1/4 cup	skim milk powder	50 mL
1 tsp	salt	5 mL
2 tbsp	granulated sugar	25 mL
2 tbsp	shortening	25 mL
3 cups	all-purpose flour or bread flour	750 mL
1/2 tsp	cinnamon	2 mL
1/4 tsp	nutmeg	1 mL
1 tsp	bread machine yeast	5 mL
1/3 cup	chopped pecans	75 mL
1/4 cup	raisins	50 mL

2 LB (1 KG)		
3/4 cup	water	175 mL
2/3 cup	mashed sweet potato	150 mL
2/3 cup	chopped apple	150 mL
1/4 cup	skim milk powder	50 mL
1 1/2 tsp	salt	8 mL
3 tbsp	granulated sugar	45 mL
3 tbsp	shortening	45 mL
3 1/2 cups	all-purpose flour or bread flour	875 mL
1 tsp	cinnamon	5 mL
1/2 tsp	nutmeg	2 mL
1 1/4 tsp	bread machine yeast	6 mL
1/2 cup	chopped pecans	125 mL
1/3 cup	raisins	75 mL

This sweet autumn bread, studded with apple pieces and pecans, is perfect with a bowl of steaming hot soup on a crisp fall day.

TIP

Choose firm, blemish-free sweet potatoes. Cutting out blemishes may not eliminate an off taste.

To increase the height of the loaf, be sure sweet potato is at room temperature.

VARIATION

Substitute canned yams for the cooked sweet potatoes. The loaf, although slightly different, is still delicious.

1. Measure all ingredients *except pecans and raisins* into baking pan in the order recommended by the manufacturer. Insert pan into the oven chamber.
2. Select **Sweet Cycle**.
3. Add pecans and raisins at "add ingredient" signal.

AUTUMN PUMPKIN SEED BREAD (PAGE 114) ➤
OVERLEAF: ASSORTMENT OF ROLLS (PAGES 81-96)

Whole Wheat Flax Seed Bread

1.5 LB (750 G)		
1 1/4 cups	water	300 mL
1/4 cup	skim milk powder	50 mL
1 1/4 tsp	salt	6 mL
1 tbsp	packed brown sugar	15 mL
2 tbsp	shortening	25 mL
3 cups	whole wheat flour	750 mL
1/2 cup	flax seeds	125 mL
1 tsp	bread machine yeast	5 mL

2 LB (1 KG)		
1 1/2 cups	water	375 mL
1/4 cup	skim milk powder	50 mL
1 1/2 tsp	salt	7 mL
2 tbsp	packed brown sugar	25 mL
2 tbsp	shortening	25 mL
3 1/2 cups	whole wheat flour	875 mL
3/4 cup	flax seeds	175 mL
1 1/2 tsp	bread machine yeast	7 mL

1. Measure ingredients into baking pan in the order recommended by the manufacturer. Insert pan into the oven chamber.
2. Select **Whole Wheat Cycle.**

Here's a crunchy, nutty, whole wheat loaf that's loaded with flax seeds.

TIP

Flax seeds can aid in lowering cholesterol levels.

VARIATION

For a lighter-textured loaf, substitute 1 cup (250 mL) all-purpose or bread flour for 1 cup (250 mL) of the whole wheat flour.

≺ GIANT PECAN STICKY BUNS (PAGE 164)

Whole Wheat Harvest Seed Bread

This variation of our COUNTRY HARVEST BREAD *is for the true whole wheat lover.*

TIP

Store flax, sesame and sunflower seeds in the refrigerator to keep them fresh.

VARIATION

For an interesting flavor, substitute 1/4 cup (50 mL) of rye flour for 1/4 cup (50 mL) of the whole wheat flour.

1.5 LB (750 G)		
1 1/4 cups	water	300 mL
1 1/2 tsp	salt	7 mL
2 tbsp	packed brown sugar	25 mL
2 tbsp	vegetable oil	25 mL
2 3/4 cups	whole wheat flour	675 mL
1/3 cup	buttermilk powder	75 mL
1/4 cup	flax seeds	50 mL
1/4 cup	sesame seeds	50 mL
1/4 cup	sunflower seeds raw, unsalted	50 mL
1 1/4 tsp	bread machine yeast	6 mL

2 LB (1 KG)		
1 1/3 cups	water	325 mL
1 1/2 tsp	salt	7 mL
3 tbsp	packed brown sugar	45 mL
3 tbsp	vegetable oil	45 mL
3 1/2 cups	whole wheat flour	875 mL
1/2 cup	buttermilk powder	125 mL
1/3 cup	flax seeds	75 mL
1/3 cup	sesame seeds	75 mL
1/3 cup	sunflower seeds raw, unsalted	75 mL
1 1/2 tsp	bread machine yeast	7 mL

1. Measure ingredients into baking pan in the order recommended by the manufacturer. Insert pan into the oven chamber.
2. Select **Whole Wheat Cycle**.

COFFEE CAKES

*Hosting a baby shower, welcoming new neighbors or
relaxing on a weekend afternoon at the cottage
they're all excellent excuses for serving an oven-fresh
coffee cake!*

Apricot Walnut Coffee Cake

MAKES 1 COFFEE CAKE		
Preheat oven to 375° F (190° C)		
Baking sheet, lightly greased		
3/4 cup	peach or apricot yogurt	175 mL
1/3 cup	water	75 mL
1	egg	1
3/4 tsp	salt	3 mL
1/4 cup	granulated sugar	50 mL
2 tbsp	butter	25 mL
3 1/3 cups	all-purpose flour or bread flour	825 mL
1 1/2 tsp	bread machine yeast	7 mL

APRICOT WALNUT FILLING		
1/4 cup	packed brown sugar	50 mL
1/2 tsp	cinnamon	2 mL
1 cup	finely chopped dried apricots	250 mL
3/4 cup	finely chopped walnuts	175 mL
1/4 cup	soft butter	50 mL

APRICOT GLAZE		
1/4 cup	apricot jam	50 mL

Welcome new neighbors with this fresh-from-the-oven coffee cake.

TIP

Snip dried apricots into 1/4-inch (5 mm) pieces with sharp scissors.

VARIATION

Substitute chopped fresh dates or dried apples for half of the apricots in this filling.

1. Measure ingredients into baking pan in the order recommended by the manufacturer. Insert pan into the oven chamber. Select **Dough Cycle**.

2. Prepare filling: In a bowl combine brown sugar and cinnamon. Toss gently with apricots and walnuts; set aside.

3. Remove dough to a lightly floured board; cover with a large bowl and let rest for 10 to 15 minutes. Roll out the dough a 16- by 8-inch (40 by 20 cm) rectangle.

4. Spread softened butter over dough; sprinkle with two-thirds of the filling. Roll jellyroll style. Using sharp scissors, cut the roll in half lengthwise. Beginning in the center of prepared baking sheet, loosely coil 1 strip of dough, cut-side up. Loosely coil the second strip of dough around the first strip, tucking the end under. Sprinkle with the remaining filling.

5. Cover and let rise in a warm, draft-free place for 30 to 45 minutes or until doubled in volume.

6. Bake in preheated oven for 35 to 40 minutes or until coffee cake sounds hollow when tapped on the bottom. If necessary, cover loosely with foil for the last 10 to 15 minutes to prevent excess browning.

7. Prepare glaze: Warm apricot jam and drizzle over warm coffee cake.

TIPS FOR HANDLING COFFEE CAKES

Here are a few suggestions for keeping coffee cakes fresh.

1. Cooling

Remove coffee cake from the pan as soon as it is baked. Turn right side up and cool completely on a wire rack before wrapping air-tight.

2. Freezing

Coffee cakes freeze well. Make several, divide into quarters or eighths and then freeze in mix-and-match packages. Wrap air-tight in plastic wrap and then over-wrap with either aluminum foil or place in zippered plastic bags. For individual servings, cut and wrap in plastic, then place in air-tight freezer bags. Freeze, un-iced, for up to 6 weeks.

3. Thawing

To prevent the coffee cake from drying out, thaw in the refrigerator, wrapped in the original wrapper.

4. Icing/Glazing

For a more attractive finish, ice and decorate with slivered nuts and fruit after thawing.

Blueberry Nutmeg Round with Lemon Glaze

MAKES **2** ROUNDS		

Preheat oven to 375° F (190° C)
10-inch (25 cm) spring form pan, lightly greased

1 1/4 cups	sour cream	300 mL
2 tsp	lemon juice	10 mL
2	eggs	2
3/4 tsp	salt	4 mL
1/4 cup	honey	50 mL
2 tbsp	butter	25 mL
3 3/4 cups	all-purpose flour or bread flour	925 mL
1/4 tsp	ground allspice	2 mL
2 tsp	lemon zest	10 mL
1 1/4 tsp	bread machine yeast	6 mL

BLUEBERRY FILLING		
4 cups	fresh blueberries	1 L
4 tsp	lemon zest	20 mL
1/2 tsp	ground allspice	2 mL

LEMON GLAZE		
1 cup	sifted icing sugar	250 mL
4 to 5 tsp	fresh lemon juice	20 to 25 mL

Freshly picked blueberries make this coffee cake a special treat.

TIP

Thawed frozen blueberries or pie filling can be substituted for the freshly picked. You may need to adjust the amount of sugar in the filling. Taste the berries and sweeten if necessary.

VARIATION

Substitute other seasonal fruits, such as raspberries or strawberries, for the blueberries.

1. Measure ingredients into baking pan in the order recommended by the manufacturer. Insert pan into the oven chamber. Select **Dough Cycle**.

2. Prepare filling: In a bowl combine filling ingredients; set aside.

3. Remove dough to a lightly floured board; cover with a large bowl and let rest for 10 to 15 minutes. Divide dough in half. Stretch each half into prepared pan. Make a cut around the entire edge, 1 inch (2.5 cm) deep and 3/4 inch (1.5 cm) from the edge.

4. Sprinkle half the filling over inner circle of each piece of dough. Cover and let rise in a warm, draft-free place for 30 to 45 minutes or until doubled in volume.

5. Bake in preheated oven for 35 to 40 minutes or until coffee cake sounds hollow when tapped on the bottom. If necessary, cover loosely with foil for the last 10 to 15 minutes to prevent excess browning.

6 Prepare glaze: In a bowl stir together glaze ingredients until smooth. Drizzle over warm coffee cakes.

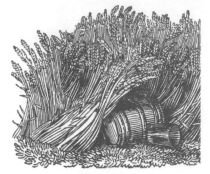

Dutch Apple Coffee Cake with Cinnamon Streusel Topping

MAKES 1 CAKE		

Preheat oven to 375° F (190° C)
13- by 9-inch (3 L) baking pan, lightly greased

1 cup	milk	250 mL
1/4 cup	unsweetened applesauce	50 mL
1	egg	1
3/4 tsp	salt	3 mL
1/4 cup	granulated sugar	50 mL
2 tbsp	butter	25 mL
3 1/2 cups	all-purpose flour or bread flour	900 mL
1 1/4 tsp	bread machine yeast	6 mL

APPLE FILLING		
3	Granny Smith apples, cut into 1/2-inch (1 cm) wedges	3
1/4 cup	packed brown sugar	50 mL
1 tsp	cinnamon	2 mL

STREUSEL TOPPING		
2 tbsp	soft butter	25 mL
1/4 cup	flour	50 mL
1/4 cup	packed brown sugar	50 mL
2 tbsp	slivered almonds	25 mL
1/4 tsp	cinnamon	1 mL

Serve this autumn treat warm accompanied by a wedge of aged Cheddar cheese.

TIP

Press apple wedges firmly into the dough to keep them in place during rising and baking.

VARIATION

Substitute 1 cup (250 mL) fresh or thawed frozen cranberries for the apples in the filling and topping.

1. Measure ingredients into baking pan in the order recommended by the manufacturer. Insert pan into the oven chamber. Select **Dough Cycle**.

2. Prepare filling: In a bowl gently toss together filling ingredients; set aside.

3. Remove dough to a lightly floured board; cover with a large bowl and let rest for 10 to 15 minutes. Divide dough in half. Roll out each into a 13- by 9-inch (33 by 22.5 cm) rectangle.

4. Place one rectangle of dough in prepared pan. Press half the apple filling mixture into the dough in lengthwise rows. Gently top with the remaining dough. Press remaining filling mixture into dough in lengthwise rows.

5. Prepare streusel topping: In a bowl combine topping ingredients. Sprinkle evenly over both cakes. Cover and let rise in a warm, draft-free place for 30 to 45 minutes or until doubled in volume.

6. Bake in preheated oven for 35 to 40 minutes or until coffee cake sounds hollow when tapped on the bottom. If necessary, cover loosely with foil for the last 10 to 15 minutes to prevent excess browning.

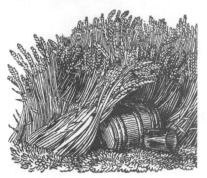

Hazelnut Plum Ladder Loaf

MAKES 2 LOAVES		

Preheat oven to 375° F (190° C)
Baking sheet, lightly greased

1 1/4 cups	milk	300 mL
1	egg	1
3/4 tsp	salt	4 mL
1/4 cup	granulated sugar	50 mL
2 tbsp	butter	25 mL
3 3/4 cups	all-purpose flour or bread flour	925 mL
1 1/4 tsp	bread machine yeast	6 mL

HAZELNUT PLUM FILLING		
2 cups	ripe plums pitted and halved	500 mL
1/2 cup	sliced hazelnuts	125 mL

STREUSEL TOPPING		
2 tbsp	flour	25 mL
2 tbsp	slivered hazelnuts	25 mL
1 tbsp	packed brown sugar	15 mL
1 tbsp	soft butter	15 mL
1/4 tsp	nutmeg	1 mL

Late fall is the perfect time to find fresh plums. This coffee cake complements a café latte or the raspberry aroma of a café leray.

TIP

For a deep plum color and flavor, use red or purple varieties of sweet plums

VARIATION

When fresh plums are unavailable, substitute a high quality plum preserve or a commercial pie filling, either "Double Fruit" or "Extra Light" varieties.

1. Measure ingredients into baking pan in the order recommended by the manufacturer. Insert pan into the oven chamber. Select **Dough Cycle**.

2. Prepare filling: In a bowl gently combine plums and hazelnuts; set aside.

3. Remove dough to a lightly floured board; cover with a large bowl and let rest for 10 to 15 minutes. Divide dough in half. Roll out each half into an 18-by 9-inch (45 by 22.5 cm) rectangle.

4. Spread half of the filling ingredients in a 3-inch (7.5 cm) wide strip lengthwise down center third of rectangle. With scissors, snip diagonally from edge of dough to edge of filling. Make cuts 3 inches (7.5 cm) long and 1 inch (2.5 cm) apart along both sides of rectangle. Fold strips over filling, alternating sides. Tuck in ends. Place on prepared baking sheet. Repeat with the second half of dough.

5. Cover and let rise in a warm, draft-free place for 30 to 45 minutes or until doubled in volume.

6. Prepare streusel topping: Mix topping ingredients and sprinkle over the risen dough.

7. Bake in preheated oven for 35 to 40 minutes or until loaves sound hollow when tapped on the bottom. If necessary, cover loosely with foil for the last 10 to 15 minutes to prevent excess browning.

Orange Braid with Poppy Seed Filling

Glazed with orange and dotted with pockets of poppy seeds, this coffee cake is moist and delicious.

TIP

To grind poppy seeds, place in a blender for 2 to 3 minutes, scraping down sides frequently.

VARIATION

Purchase a ready-made filling, then add the fruit, nuts and zest.

MAKES 1 BRAID		

Preheat oven to 375° F (190° C)
Baking sheet, lightly greased

3/4 cup	milk	175 mL
1/2 cup	orange juice	125 mL
1	egg	1
3/4 tsp	salt	3 mL
1/4 cup	packed brown sugar	50 mL
2 tbsp	butter	25 mL
3 3/4 cups	all-purpose flour or bread flour	950 mL
2 tsp	orange zest	10 mL
1 1/4 tsp	bread machine yeast	6 mL

POPPY SEED FILLING		
3/4 cup	ground poppy seeds	175 mL
1/2 cup	granulated sugar	125 mL
3/4 cup	milk	175 mL
1 tsp	almond extract	5 mL
1	egg white, slightly beaten	1
1/2 cup	raisins	125 mL
1/2 cup	chopped pecans	125 mL
2 tsp	lemon zest	10 mL

1. Measure ingredients into baking pan in the order recommended by the manufacturer. Insert pan into the oven chamber. Select **Dough Cycle**.

2. Prepare filling: In a saucepan over low heat, combine poppy seeds, sugar and milk; cook, stirring, for about 15 minutes or until thick. Cool slightly. Add almond extract and egg white. Stir in raisins, pecans and lemon zest. Set aside and allow to cool.

3. Remove dough to a lightly floured board; cover with a large bowl and let rest for 10 to 15 minutes. Divide dough into thirds. Roll out each into an 18- by 3-inch (45 by 7.5 cm) rectangle.

4. Spread one-third of the filling down center of each portion to within 1/2 inch (1 cm) of ends and edges. Pinch dough together. On floured board, roll each into a smooth rope. Braid, tucking under the ends. Place on prepared baking sheet.

5. Cover and let rise in a warm, draft-free place for 30 to 45 minutes or until doubled in volume.

6. Bake in preheated oven for 35 to 40 minutes or until braid sounds hollow when tapped on the bottom. If necessary, cover loosely with foil for the last 10 to 15 minutes to prevent excess browning.

Raspberry Almond Streusel Coffee Cake

The Swedes are coffee cake lovers, enjoying baked sweets, rich in almonds, with their coffee. Enjoy this tradition with our streusel coffee cake.

VARIATION

Choose a "lite" double fruit jam for the freshest taste.

MAKES 1 COFFEE CAKE		

Preheat oven to 375° F (190° C)
13- by 9-inch (3 L) baking dish, lightly greased

1 1/4 cups	milk	300 mL
1	egg	1
3/4 tsp	salt	3 mL
1/4 cup	granulated sugar	50 mL
2 tbsp	butter	25 mL
3 3/4 cups	all-purpose flour or bread flour	925 mL
1 1/4 tsp	bread machine yeast	6 mL

RASPBERRY FILLING		
1/4 to 1/3 cup	raspberry jam	50 to 75 mL

STREUSEL TOPPING		
2 tbsp	soft butter	25 mL
1/4 cup	all-purpose flour	50 mL
1/4 cup	chopped pecans	50 mL
2 tbsp	packed brown sugar	25 mL
1/2 tsp	nutmeg	2 mL

1. Measure ingredients into baking pan in the order recommended by the manufacturer. Insert pan into the oven chamber. Select **Dough Cycle**.

2. Prepare filling: In a bowl combine topping ingredients until crumbly; set aside.

3. Remove dough to a lightly floured board; cover with a large bowl and let rest for 10 to 15 minutes. Press dough into prepared baking dish.

4. With the handle of a wooden spoon, press holes into the dough three-quarters of the way through. Do not press to the bottom of the pan. Fill each hole with a 1/4 tsp (1 mL) of raspberry jam.

5. Sprinkle prepared streusel topping over coffee cake. Cover and let rise in a warm, draft-free place for 30 to 45 minutes or until doubled in volume.

6. Bake in preheated oven for 35 to 40 minutes or until coffee cake sounds hollow when tapped on the bottom. If necessary, cover loosely with foil for the last 10 to 15 minutes to prevent excess browning.

Savory Cheese Twist

MAKES 1 TWIST		

Preheat oven to 350° F (180° C)
Baking sheet, lightly greased

1 cup	water	250 mL
1/2 cup	cottage cheese	125 mL
1	egg	1
3/4 tsp	salt	3 mL
2 tbsp	granulated sugar	25 mL
2 tbsp	butter	25 mL
3 1/2 cups	all-purpose flour or bread flour	875 mL
1 1/4 tsp	bread machine yeast	6 mL

CHEESE FILLING		
3/4 cup	shredded Havarti cheese	175 mL
3/4 cup	shredded Monterey Jack	175 mL
1/4 cup	grated Parmesan cheese	50 mL

Serve this savory twist with a chef's salad for lunch or as a mid-morning treat with a crisp red apple and a glass of cold milk.

TIP

For a better blend of flavors, mix the grated cheeses well.

VARIATION

Try a combination of Asiago, Monterey Jack and feta — or any other cheese your family enjoys.

1. Measure ingredients into baking pan in the order recommended by the manufacturer. Insert pan into the oven chamber. Select **Dough Cycle**.

2. Prepare filling: In a bowl combine filling ingredients until well mixed; set aside.

3. Remove dough to a lightly floured board; cover with a large bowl and let rest for 10 to 15 minutes. Roll out dough into an 18- by 12-inch (45 by 30 cm) rectangle.

4. Sprinkle filling evenly over dough to within 1/2 inch (1 cm) of edges. Beginning at a long end, roll up tightly. Place seam-side down on prepared baking sheet. With scissors, cut lengthwise down the center of roll, about 1 inch (5 cm) deep and to within 1/2 inch (1 cm) of ends. Keeping cut sides up, form into an "S."

5. Cover and let rise in a warm, draft-free place for 30 to 45 minutes or until doubled in volume.

6. Bake in preheated oven for 35 to 40 minutes or until twist sounds hollow when tapped on the bottom. If necessary, cover loosely with foil for the last 10 to 15 minutes to prevent excess browning.

Springtime Rhubarb Crunch Coffee Cake

MAKES 1 COFFEE CAKE

Preheat oven to 375° F (190° C)
13- by 9-inch (3 L) baking pan, lightly greased

1 cup	milk	250 mL
1	egg	1
3/4 tsp	salt	3 mL
1/4 cup	granulated sugar	50 mL
2 tbsp	butter	25 mL
3 1/4 cups	all-purpose flour or bread flour	800 mL
1 tsp	bread machine yeast	5 mL

RHUBARB FILLING

5 cups	fresh or frozen thawed rhubarb chunks	1.25 L
1/3 cup	all-purpose flour or bread flour	75 mL
3/4 cup	granulated sugar	175 mL
2 tsp	lemon zest	10 mL

OATMEAL TOPPING

1 1/2 cups	rolled oats	375 mL
1/3 cup	packed brown sugar	75 mL
1/4 cup	soft butter	50 mL
1 tsp	nutmeg	5 mL

The first harvest of rhubarb heralds the arrival of spring. Here its tart flavor is combined with oatmeal, giving this coffee cake added crunch.

TIP

For the most attractive filling, choose thin stalks of ruby red strawberry rhubarb.

VARIATION

Substitute fresh or frozen thawed strawberries for half the rhubarb.

1. Measure ingredients into baking pan in the order recommended by the manufacturer. Insert pan into the oven chamber. Select **Dough Cycle**.

2. Prepare filling: In a small saucepan over low heat, combine rhubarb and flour; cook until tender. (Or combine in a bowl and cook in microwave.) Drain excess liquid. Add sugar and lemon zest; stir to dissolve sugar. Cool before using; set aside.

Recipe continues on following page…

3. Remove dough to a lightly floured board; cover with a large bowl and let rest for 10 to 15 minutes. Stretch into prepared baking pan.
4. Spread filling evenly over dough to within 1/2 inch (1 cm) of the edges.
5. Prepare oatmeal topping: In a bowl combine topping ingredients until well mixed; sprinkle over cake.
6. Cover and let rise in a warm, draft-free place for 30 to 45 minutes or until doubled in volume.
7. Bake in preheated oven for 35 to 40 minutes or until cake sounds hollow when tapped on the bottom. If necessary, cover loosely with foil for the last 10 to 15 minutes to prevent excess browning.

GLAZES AND ICINGS

Drizzle glaze over cakes while they are still warm. It will coat and drip attractively down the edges of the cake. If the cake is too hot, however, the glaze will simply disappear into the cake. Before applying icings, baked goods should cool completely. Use a pastry tube for creative icing patterns.

Try some of these glazes and icing:

CINNAMON STREUSEL

Combine until crumbly 1/4 cup (50 mL) soft butter, 1/4 cup (50 mL) packed brown sugar, 1/4 cup (50 mL) flour, 1/3 cup (75 mL) raisins and 1/2 tsp (2 mL) cinnamon.

ALMOND GLAZE

Combine until smooth 3/4 cup (175 mL) icing sugar, 4 to 5 tsp (20 to 25 mL) milk and 1/4 tsp (1 mL) almond extract.

ORANGE GLAZE

Combine until smooth 1 cup (250 mL) sifted icing sugar and 4 to 5 tsp (20 to 25 mL) orange juice concentrate.

CORN SYRUP GLAZE

For a sticky bun taste, brush with 2 tbsp (25 mL) corn syrup, just before baking.

LEMON GLAZE

Combine until smooth 1 cup (250 mL) icing sugar and 4 to 5 tsp (20 to 25 mL) fresh lemon juice.

DESSERT, ANYONE?

Sweet bread recipes calling for milk, eggs and butter provide the extra-rich flavor we enjoy for dessert. Their warm, golden crusts and sweet fragrance will greet you as you open the lid of the bread machine.

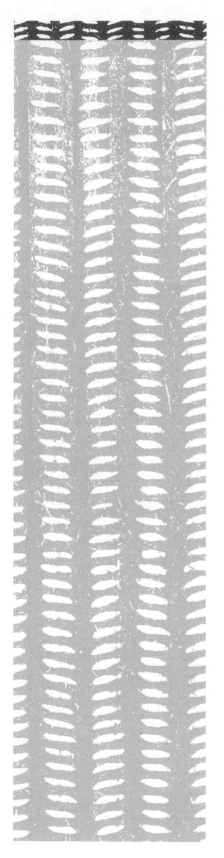

TIPS FOR A TERRIFIC LOAF

1. For a more tender loaf, use homogenized or 2% milk rather than water.

2. Check your bread machine's manual. If it does not have a preheat cycle or requires liquids at room temperature, microwave the milk until just lukewarm; if it's too hot, it will kill the yeast.

3. Butter at room temperature should be measured in little dollops, not one big clump, when adding with the other ingredients to the baking pan.

4. Large amounts of pumpkin, sweet potato or applesauce should be warmed to room temperature before adding.

5. Eggs should be large and used straight from the refrigerator.

6. Loaves containing milk, butter, eggs and other perishables should not be prepared using the timer.

7. Add raisins and fruit at the "add ingredients" signal. If your bread machine doesn't have this feature, check your manual to determine the time to add them. The time is important; too early and the fruit breaks up and is puréed; too late and it sits on the outside and could have a burnt taste.

8. Nuts, whole dates and chocolate chips can be added with the dry ingredients.

9. Keep cinnamon away from yeast; it slows down the rising action.

Orange Pecan Loaf

1.5 LB (750 G)		
1 1/4 cups	water	300 mL
2 tbsp	frozen orange juice concentrate, thawed	25 mL
1/4 tsp	orange extract	1 mL
1 1/4 tsp	salt	6 mL
2 tbsp	granulated sugar	25 mL
2 tbsp	shortening	25 mL
3 1/3 cups	all-purpose flour or bread flour	850 mL
1/2 cup	chopped pecans	125 mL
2 tsp	orange zest	10 mL
1 tsp	cinnamon	5 mL
1 tsp	bread machine yeast	5 mL

2 LB (1 KG)		L
1 1/3 cups	water	325 mL
1/4 cup	frozen orange juice concentrate, thawed	50 mL
1/2 tsp	orange extract	2 mL
1 1/2 tsp	salt	7 mL
3 tbsp	granulated sugar	45 mL
2 tbsp	shortening	25 mL
3 3/4 cups	all-purpose flour or bread flour	950 mL
2/3 cup	chopped pecans	150 mL
1 tbsp	orange zest	15 mL
1 tsp	cinnamon	5 mL
1 1/4 tsp	bread machine yeast	6 mL

A triple-orange aroma greets you as you open the bread machine lid. The orange flavor enhances every bite.

TIP

To thaw frozen orange juice remove lid from container; microwave 20 seconds on High. This way you can scoop out the juice without thawing the whole container.

VARIATION

For a mixed citrus flavor, substitute lemon extract for the orange extract.

1. Measure ingredients into baking pan in the order recommended by the manufacturer. Insert pan into the oven chamber.
2. Select **Sweet Cycle**.

Apricot Pecan Twists

MAKES 20 TWISTS		

Preheat oven to 350° F (180° C)
Baking sheet, lightly greased

1 1/4 cups	milk	300 mL
1	egg	1
3/4 tsp	salt	3 mL
1/4 cup	granulated sugar	50 mL
2 tbsp	butter	25 mL
3 3/4 cups	all-purpose flour or bread flour	950 mL
1 1/4 tsp	bread machine yeast	6 mL

APRICOT PECAN FILLING		
1/2 cup	packed brown sugar	125 mL
1/2 tsp	cinnamon	2 mL
2/3 cup	finely chopped dried apricots	150 mL
2/3 cup	finely chopped pecans	150 mL
1/4 cup	melted butter, cooled	50 mL

ORANGE GLAZE		
1 cup	sifted icing sugar	250 mL
4 to 5 tsp	frozen orange juice concentrate, thawed	20 to 25 mL

With their tart golden chunks of apricot peeking out between the twists of dough, you'll be tempted to taste these fingers hot from the oven.

TIP

Press the ends flat to prevent them from untwisting on the baking sheet.

VARIATION

To please the younger lunchbox set, substitute the sweeter flavors of apple or cherry for the apricots.

1. Measure dough ingredients into baking pan in the order recommended by the manufacturer. Insert pan into the oven chamber. Select **Dough Cycle**.

2. Prepare filling. In a bowl combine brown sugar and cinnamon. Toss gently with apricots and pecans; set aside. Let melted butter cool slightly; set aside.

3. Remove dough to a lightly floured board; cover with a large bowl and let rest for 10 to 15 minutes. Divide dough in half. Roll out each half into a 12-inch (30 cm) square.

4. Brush one square with half the melted butter. Sprinkle half the filling over half the dough. Fold over the other half and carefully pinch to seal. Cut crosswise into ten strips, 6 inches (15 cm) long. Twist each strip twice. Place on prepared baking sheet. Repeat procedure with remaining square of dough.

5. Cover and let rise in a warm, draft-free place for 30 to 45 minutes or until doubled in volume.

6. Bake in preheated oven for 12 to 15 minutes or until twists sound hollow when tapped on the bottom.

7. Prepare glaze. In a bowl stir together glaze ingredients until smooth. Drizzle over warm twists.

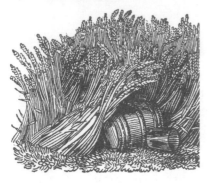

Banana Pecan Sticky Buns

MAKES 9 BUNS		

Preheat oven to 350° F (180° C)
8 inch (2 L) baking pan, lightly greased

1 cup	mashed ripe bananas	250 mL
2	egg whites	2
1/4 cup	skim milk powder	50 mL
1/2 tsp	salt	2 mL
3 tbsp	granulated sugar	45 mL
2 tbsp	shortening	25 mL
1 cup	whole wheat flour	250 mL
2 cups	all-purpose flour or bread flour	500 mL
2 tsp	bread machine yeast	10 mL

FILLING		
2 tbsp	soft butter	25 mL
1/4 cup	packed brown sugar	50 mL
1/2 tsp	cinnamon	2 mL
3/4 cup	raisins	175 mL

PAN GLAZE		
1/4 cup	maple syrup	50 mL
1/2 cup	chopped pecans	125 mL

Enjoy the aroma of banana as you tip the dough out of the baking pan to form these sticky buns.

TIP

Corn syrup can be substituted for the maple syrup in the pan glaze.

VARIATION

Use all-purpose flour or bread flour instead of the whole wheat.

For a change, try coffee icing. Use a basic icing recipe and substitute cold coffee for the milk.

1. Measure dough ingredients into baking pan in the order recommended by the manufacturer. Insert pan into the oven chamber. Select **Dough Cycle**.

2. Prepare filling: In a bowl combine brown sugar, cinnamon and raisins; set aside. Prepare pan glaze: In a bowl combine glaze ingredients and spread in prepared pan; set aside.

3. Remove dough to a lightly floured board; cover with a large bowl and let rest for 10 to 15 minutes. Roll out dough to a 14- by 9-inch (35 by 22.5 cm) rectangle.

4. Spread dough with soft butter to within 1/2 inch (1 cm) of the edges. Sprinkle filling over the dough. Beginning at the long side, roll jellyroll style. Pinch to seal seam. Cut into 9 pieces 1 1/2 inches (3.5 cm) wide.

5. Arrange the buns, cut-side up, in prepared pan; cover and let rise in a warm, draft-free place for 30 to 45 minutes or until doubled in volume.

6. Bake in preheated oven for 25 to 35 minutes or until buns sound hollow when tapped on the bottom.

7. Immediately turn upside down on a serving platter. Allow to stand for 5 minutes before removing pan.

Black Forest Loaf

1.5 LB (750 G)		
3/4 cup	milk	175 mL
1 tbsp	brandy	15 mL
1	egg	1
1 1/2 tsp	salt	7 mL
2 tbsp	honey	25 mL
2 tbsp	butter	25 mL
2 1/2 cups	all-purpose flour or bread flour	625 mL
1 1/4 tsp	bread machine yeast	6 mL
1/2 cup	semi-sweet chocolate chips	125 mL
1/2 cup	dried cherries	125 mL

This not-too-sweet loaf is studded with bits of semi-sweet chocolate and dried cherries, with a hint of brandy to heighten the flavor.

TIP

For a lighter-textured loaf, warm milk to room temperature.

VARIATION

Add large chocolate chunks at the "add ingredient" signal. Depending on the brand of bread machine, your loaf may turn out marbled.

2 LB (1 KG)		
1 cup	milk	250 mL
2 tbsp	brandy	25 mL
1	egg	1
1 1/2 tsp	salt	7 mL
3 tbsp	honey	45 mL
2 tbsp	butter	25 mL
3 1/2 cups	all-purpose flour or bread flour	875 mL
1 1/2 tsp	bread machine yeast	7 mL
2/3 cup	semi-sweet chocolate chips	150 mL
2/3 cup	dried cherries	150 mL

1. Measure all ingredients *except chocolate chips and cherries* into baking pan in the order recommended by the manufacturer. Insert pan into the oven chamber.
2. Select **Sweet Cycle**.
3. Add chocolate chips and dried cherries at the "add ingredient" signal.

Chocolate Banana Loaf

1.5 LB (750 G)		
1 1/4 cups	mashed bananas	300 mL
1	egg	1
1/4 cup	skim milk powder	50 mL
1 1/4 tsp	salt	6 mL
1 tbsp	honey	15 mL
1 tbsp	butter	15 mL
3 cups	all-purpose flour or bread flour	750 mL
1/3 cup	chocolate chips	75 mL
1 1/2 tsp	bread machine yeast	7 mL

2 LB (1 KG)		
1 1/2 cups	mashed bananas	325 mL
2	eggs	2
1 1/2 tsp	salt	7 mL
1/4 cup	skim milk powder	50 mL
2 tbsp	honey	25 mL
2 tbsp	butter	25 mL
3 1/4 cups	all-purpose flour or bread flour	800 mL
1/2 cup	chocolate chips	125 mL
1 1/2 tsp	bread machine yeast	7 mL

A child's dream combination — bananas and chocolate! Serve with a glass of cold milk and the after-school snack is complete.

TIP

Freeze mashed overripe bananas in 1-cup (250 mL) containers. Thaw and bring to room temperature before adding.

VARIATION

Substitute peanut butter chips for the chocolate chips and add 1/2 cup (125 mL) shelled unsalted peanuts.

1. Measure ingredients into baking pan in the order recommended by the manufacturer. Insert pan into the oven chamber.
2. Select **Sweet Cycle**.

Chocolate Fudge Loaf

1.5 LB (750 G)		
1 cup	water	250 mL
1 oz	bittersweet chocolate, melted and cooled	30 g
1	egg	1
1 1/2 tsp	salt	7 mL
3 tbsp	honey	45 mL
3 cups	all-purpose flour or bread flour	750 mL
1/3 cup	buttermilk powder	75 mL
2 tbsp	cocoa	25 mL
1 1/2 tsp	bread machine yeast	7 mL
1/2 cup	chocolate chips	125 mL

2 LB (1 KG)		
1 1/4 cups	water	300 mL
1 1/2 oz	bittersweet chocolate, melted and cooled	40 g
1	egg	1
1 1/2 tsp	salt	7 mL
1/4 cup	honey	50 mL
3 1/2 cups	all-purpose flour or bread flour	875 mL
1/2 cup	buttermilk powder	125 mL
3 tbsp	cocoa	45 mL
1 1/2 tsp	bread machine yeast	7 mL
3/4 cup	chocolate chips	125mL

Double the goodness with double the chocolate.

TIP

If there are no chocolate squares in the cupboard, substitute 3 tbsp (45 mL) cocoa, and 1 tbsp (15 mL) butter for each 1 oz (30 g) square.

To melt chocolate, cut square in half; microwave on 50% power, just until soft.

VARIATION

Try 1/2 cup (125 mL) mint or white chocolate chips for a change.

1. Measure all ingredients *except chocolate chips* into baking pan in the order recommended by the manufacturer. Insert pan into the oven chamber.
2. Select **Sweet Cycle**.
3. Add chocolate chips at the "add ingredient" signal.

Chop Suey Loaf

Chockfull of mixed candied fruit and peel, this is an old stand-by. Drizzle with lemon icing and serve thinly sliced or toasted.

TIP

For a lighter, less-sweet loaf, rinse the candied fruit under cold water and dry well before adding to the baking pan.

VARIATION

This recipe can become a Russian Kulich by substituting part of the fruit with the same amount of raisins and toasted almonds.

1.5 LB (750 G)		
3/4 cup	water	175 mL
1	egg	1
1/4 cup	skim milk powder	50 mL
1 1/4 tsp	salt	6 mL
2 tbsp	granulated sugar	25 mL
2 tbsp	butter	25 mL
2 1/3 cups	all-purpose flour or bread flour	575 mL
1 1/4 tsp	bread machine yeast	6 mL
1 cup	mixed candied fruit	250 mL
1/4 cup	raisins	50 mL

2 LB (1 KG)		
1 cup	water	250 mL
2	eggs	2
1/4 cup	skim milk powder	50 mL
1 1/2 tsp	salt	7 mL
2 tbsp	granulated sugar	25 mL
2 tbsp	butter	25 mL
3 1/2 cups	all-purpose flour or bread flour	825 mL
1 1/4 tsp	bread machine yeast	6 mL
1 1/2 cups	mixed candied fruit	375 mL
1/2 cup	raisins	125 mL

1. Measure all ingredients *except candied fruit and raisins* into baking pan in the order recommended by the manufacturer. Insert pan into the oven chamber.
2. Select **Sweet Cycle**.
3. Add raisins and fruit at the "add ingredient" signal.

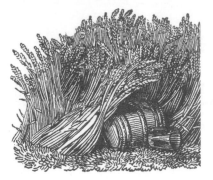

Cinnamon Nut Twists

MAKES **20** TWISTS		

Preheat oven to 350° F (180° C)
Baking sheet, lightly greased

1 1/4 cups	water	300 mL
1	egg	1
3/4 tsp	salt	3 mL
1/4 cup	honey	50 mL
2 tbsp	butter	25 mL
3 3/4 cups	all-purpose flour or bread flour	925 mL
1 1/4 tsp	bread machine yeast	6 mL

CINNAMON NUT FILLING		
3/4 cup	finely chopped walnuts	175 mL
1/2 cup	packed brown sugar	125 mL
1 tsp	cinnamon	5 mL
1/4 cup	butter	50 mL

Here's the perfect way to welcome a hungry gang of hockey players home from the Saturday morning game. Serve with a mug of hot chocolate topped with marshmallows.

TIP

To form the dough, pick up a strip with a hand at each end; twist each end in opposite directions. Press the ends onto the baking sheet to prevent it from untwisting during proofing.

VARIATION

Substitute hazelnuts for the walnuts and 1/2 tsp (2 mL) nutmeg for the cinnamon.

1. Measure dough ingredients into baking pan in the order recommended by the manufacturer. Insert pan into the oven chamber. Select **Dough Cycle**.

2. Prepare filling: Combine walnuts, brown sugar and cinnamon; set aside. Melt butter. Cool slightly before using.

3. Remove dough to a lightly floured board; cover with a large bowl and let rest for 10 to 15 minutes. Divide dough in half. Roll out each half into a 12-inch (30 cm) square.

3. Brush one square with half the melted butter. Sprinkle half of the filling mixture over half the dough. Fold over the other half and carefully pinch to seal. Cut crosswise into 10 strips, 6 inches (15 cm) long. Twist each strip twice. Place on prepared baking sheet. Cover and let rise in a warm, draft-free place for 30 to 45 minutes or until doubled in volume.

4. Bake in preheated oven for 12 to 15 minutes or until twists sound hollow when tapped on the bottom.

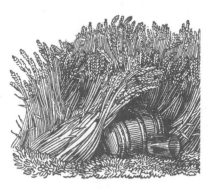

Cran-Raspberry Orange Bread

1.5 LB (750 G)		
3/4 cup	water	175 mL
1/4 cup	cran-raspberry juice	50 mL
1/4 cup	orange marmalade	50 mL
1/2 tsp	orange extract	2 mL
1/4 cup	skim milk powder	50 mL
1 1/2 tsp	salt	7 mL
1 tbsp	granulated sugar	15 mL
2 tbsp	butter	25 mL
2 3/4 cups	all-purpose flour or bread flour	675 mL
2 tsp	orange zest	10 mL
1 3/4 tsp	bread machine yeast	8 mL
1/2 cup	fresh cranberries	125 mL

2 LB (1 KG)		
1 cup	water	250 mL
1/3 cup	cran-raspberry juice	75 mL
1/3 cup	orange marmalade	75 mL
1/2 tsp	orange extract	2 mL
1/4 cup	skim milk powder	50 mL
1 1/2 tsp	salt	7 mL
2 tbsp	granulated sugar	25 mL
2 tbsp	butter	25 mL
3 1/2 cups	all-purpose flour or bread flour	875 mL
1 tbsp	orange zest	15 mL
1 3/4 tsp	bread machine yeast	8 mL
3/4 cup	fresh cranberries	175 mL

Bake this tart-but-sweet loaf at the first sign of fall, when fresh cranberries arrive in the grocery store.

TIP

Choose only unsweetened fruit juices. Fruit drinks or sweetened juices will result in a less-than-perfect loaf.

VARIATION

For a different taste treat, try other cranberry juice combinations.

1. Measure all ingredients *except cranberries* into baking pan in the order recommended by the manufacturer. Insert pan into the oven chamber.
2. Select **Sweet Cycle**.
3. Add cranberries at the "add ingredient" signal.

Cinnamon Walnut Swirl Loaf

Each slice is a perfect pinwheel. Your guests will wonder how you formed this loaf.

TIP

Poke the dough with a long skewer in several places before baking to prevent a large bubble from forming under the top crust.

VARIATION

Try this recipe with date filling: In a bowl combine 4 oz (125 g) chopped dates, 2 tbsp (25 mL) sugar and 1 tsp (5 mL) cinnamon. No need to cook this filling.

MAKES 1 LOAF		
Preheat oven to 350° F (180° C) 9- by 5-inch (2 L) loaf pan, lightly greased		
1 cup	milk	250 mL
1	egg	1
3/4 tsp	salt	3 mL
3 tbsp	granulated sugar	45 mL
2 tbsp	butter	25 mL
3 cups	all-purpose flour or bread flour	750 mL
1 1/4 tsp	bread machine yeast	6 mL

DOUBLE WALNUT FILLING		
1 cup	chopped walnuts	250 mL
3/4 cup	ground walnuts	175 mL
1/2 cup	granulated sugar	125 mL
2	egg whites	2
2 tsp	water	10 mL
1/4 tsp	cinnamon	1 mL

1. Measure ingredients into baking pan in the order recommended by the manufacturer. Insert pan into the oven chamber. Select **Dough Cycle**.

2. Prepare filling: In a saucepan over low heat, combine filling ingredients; cook, stirring, 10 minutes or until sugar dissolves. Set aside and allow to cool.

3. Remove dough to a lightly floured board; cover with a large bowl and let rest for 10 to 15 minutes. Roll out to a 16- by 8-inch (40 by 20 cm) rectangle.

4. Spread filling to within 1/2 inch (1 cm) of edges. Starting at short side, tightly roll like a jellyroll. Place in prepared pan. Cover and let rise in a warm, draft-free place for 30 to 45 minutes or until doubled in volume.

5. With a long skewer, poke several holes in risen dough. Bake in preheated oven for 40 to 50 minutes or until loaf sounds hollow when tapped on the bottom.

RASPBERRY ALMOND STREUSEL COFFEE CAKE (PAGE 142) ➤

Donuts

Preheat deep-fryer to 350° F (180° C)
Baking sheet, lightly greased

3/4 cup	water	175 mL
2	eggs	2
1/4 cup	skim milk powder	50 mL
1 tsp	salt	5 mL
1/4 cup	granulated sugar	50 mL
1/3 cup	shortening	75 mL
3 1/4 cups	all-purpose flour or bread flour	800 mL
2 tsp	bread machine yeast	10 mL

It's said that donuts were invented when a hungry boy poked his finger into his mother's round fried yeast cakes. Everybody will love these home-made delights.

TIP

To fill jelly donuts, use a pastry bag with 1/4-inch (5 mm) hole in the end; press a little jelly or pie filling into the donuts through the slit. A cookie press or cake decorator with a straight tube can be used instead of the pastry bag.

VARIATION

To make jelly donuts, cut rolled dough with a 3 1/2-inch (8 cm) round cookie cutter. Deep-fry; drain on paper towels. With a sharp, thin knife, pierce donuts from one side almost to the other and fill.

1. Measure ingredients into baking pan in the order recommended by the manufacturer. Insert pan into oven chamber. Select **Dough Cycle**.

2. Remove dough to a lightly floured board; cover with a large bowl and let rest for 10 to 15 minutes. Divide dough in half. Roll out to 1/2-inch (1 cm) thickness.

3. Cut the dough with a 3 1/2-inch (8 cm) donut cutter. Place on prepared baking sheet. Cover and let rise in a warm, draft-free place for 30 to 45 minutes or until doubled in volume.

4. Deep-fry for 30 to 45 seconds on each side, or until golden brown. Drain on paper towels. Dust warm donuts with sifted icing sugar

≺ THANKSGIVING HARVEST TWIST (PAGE 182)

Grandma's Cinnamon Raisin Bread

1.5 LB (750 G)		
1 1/4 cups	water	300 mL
1	egg	1
1/4 cup	skim milk powder	50 mL
1 1/4 tsp	salt	6 mL
2 tbsp	packed brown sugar	25 mL
2 tbsp	shortening	25 mL
3 1/2 cups	all-purpose flour or bread flour	875 mL
1 tsp	cinnamon	5 mL
3/4 tsp	bread machine yeast	4 mL
3/4 cup	raisins	150 mL

2 LB (1 KG)		
1 1/3 cups	water	325 mL
1	egg	1
1/4 cup	skim milk powder	50 mL
1 1/4 tsp	salt	6 mL
1/4 cup	packed brown sugar	50 mL
2 tbsp	shortening	25 mL
3 3/4 cups	all-purpose flour or bread flour	950 mL
1 1/2 tsp	cinnamon	7 mL
1 tsp	bread machine yeast	5 mL
1 cup	raisins	250 mL

The aroma of toasted cinnamon bread — what better way to ensure everyone arrives at the breakfast table with a smile?

TIP

For a stronger cinnamon flavor, serve with a cinnamon sugar spread. Do not increase the cinnamon called for in the recipe or the loaf will be short.

VARIATION

For an interesting taste treat, add 1/4 cup (50 mL) chopped walnuts with the raisins.

1. Measure all ingredients *except raisins* into baking pan in the order recommended by the manufacturer. Inset pan into the oven chamber.
2. Select **Sweet Cycle**.
3. Add raisins at "add ingredients" signal.

Spicy Gingerbread

1.5 LB (750 G)		
1 cup	water	250 mL
1	egg	1
1/4 cup	skim milk powder	50 mL
1 tsp	salt	5 mL
2 tbsp	packed brown sugar	25 mL
2 tbsp	molasses	25 mL
1 tbsp	shortening	15 mL
3 cups	all-purpose flour or bread flour	750 mL
3/4 tsp	ground ginger	4 mL
1/2 tsp	cinnamon	3 mL
1/4 tsp	ground cloves	2 mL
1 1/2 tsp	bread machine yeast	8 mL

2 LB (1 KG)		L
1 1/4 cups	water	300 mL
1	egg	1
1/4 cup	skim milk powder	50 mL
1 1/4 tsp	salt	6 mL
3 tbsp	packed brown sugar	45 mL
2 tbsp	molasses	25 mL
1 tbsp	shortening	15 mL
3 2/3 cups	all-purpose flour or bread flour	925 mL
1 tsp	ground ginger	5 mL
1 tsp	cinnamon	5 mL
1/2 tsp	ground cloves	2 mL
1 1/4 tsp	bread machine yeast	6 mL

1. Measure ingredients into baking pan in the order recommended by the manufacturer. Insert pan into the oven chamber.
2. Select **Sweet Cycle**.

With the sweetness of allspice, ginger and nutmeg, every bite will remind you of spice cake and gingerbread people.

TIP

Vary amounts of spices to your taste. A small amount of mace or cinnamon could be added.

VARIATION

Try this recipe with 1 cup (250 mL) raisins added at the "add ingredients" signal.

Giant Pecan Sticky Buns

MAKES 20 STICKY BUNS		

Preheat oven to 375° F (190° C)
9- by 13-inch (3 L) baking pan, lightly greased

1 cup	water	250 mL
1/4 cup	skim milk powder	50 mL
3/4 tsp	salt	3 mL
2 tbsp	packed brown sugar	25 mL
1 tbsp	shortening	15 mL
3 1/4 cups	all-purpose flour or bread flour	800 mL
3/4 tsp	bread machine yeast	3 mL

PECAN PAN GLAZE		
1/4 cup	melted butter	50 mL
1/4 cup	packed brown sugar	50 mL
1/4 cup	corn syrup	50 mL
1/2 cup	pecan halves	125 mL

RAISIN PECAN FILLING		
1 cup	raisins	250 mL
1/4 cup	chopped pecans	50 mL
1/4 cup	packed brown sugar	50 mL
1 tsp	nutmeg	5 mL
1/4 cup	soft butter	50 mL

If you need some inspiration to make these sticky buns, take a look at the picture facing page 129. You'll be in the kitchen in a minute.

TIP

Center each pecan half in the pan where you plan to set each bun.

VARIATION

Make mini-buns by rolling half the dough to a 20- by 7-inch (30 by 17.5 cm) rectangle and cutting into 1-inch (2.5 cm) slices. Shorten the baking time.

1. Measure ingredients into baking pan in the order recommended by the manufacturer. Insert pan into the oven chamber. Select **Dough Cycle**.

2. Prepare pan glaze: In a bowl combine butter, sugar and corn syrup. Spread in prepared pan. Place pecan halves, top-side down; set aside.

3. Prepare filling: In a bowl combine all filling ingredients except butter; mix well. Set aside.

4. Remove dough to a lightly floured board; cover with a large bowl and let rest 10 to 15 minutes. Divide dough in half. Roll out each half to a 20- by 7-inch (50 by 17.5 cm) rectangle.

5. Spread one rectangle with half the soft butter to within 1/2 inch (1 cm) of the edges. Sprinkle half the filling over the dough and pinch to seal. Beginning at the long side, roll jellyroll style. Pinch to seal seam. Cut into 10 pieces. Place in one half of prepared pan, cut side up. Repeat procedure with remaining dough.

6. Cover and let dough rise in a warm, draft-free place for 30 to 45 minutes or until doubled in volume.

7. Bake in preheated oven for 25 to 35 minutes or until buns sound hollow when tapped on the bottom. Immediately turn upside down on a serving platter. Allow to stand for 5 minutes before removing pan.

Sour Cherry Almond Kuchen

MAKES **2** KUCHEN		

Preheat oven to 375° F (190° C)
Baking sheet, lightly greased

1 cup	milk	250 mL
1 tsp	almond extract	5 mL
1	egg	1
1 tsp	salt	5 mL
2 tbsp	granulated sugar	25 mL
1/4 cup	butter	50 mL
3 1/2 cups	all-purpose flour or bread flour	875 mL
1 tsp	ground cardamom	5 mL
1 tsp	bread machine yeast	5 mL

ALMOND FILLING		
5 oz	almond paste	150 g
1	egg white, slightly beaten	1
1 cup	thawed frozen sour cherries, well drained	250 mL
1/2 cup	toasted slivered almonds	125 mL

Kuchen is a fruit- or cheese-filled, yeast-raised cake that originated in Germany.

TIP

Thaw frozen sour cherries completely before adding; otherwise the cold dough will take too long to rise.

Mash the almond paste with a fork. Don't worry about a few lumps; over-mixing can make the filling too runny.

VARIATION

Substitute an equal amount of fresh pitted sour cherries for the frozen. Dried sour cherries are neither as attractive nor as tasty in this recipe.

Substitute an equal amount of fresh blueberries or sliced apples for the sour cherries.

1. Measure ingredients into baking pan in the order recommended by the manufacturer. Insert pan into the oven chamber. Select **Dough Cycle**.
2. Prepare filling: In a bowl combine almond paste and egg white; mix lightly with a fork. Set aside.
3. Remove dough to a lightly floured board; cover with a large bowl and let rest for 10 to 15 minutes. Divide dough in half. Roll out each half to a 15- by 9-inch (38 by 22.5 cm) rectangle.

4. Spread one rectangle with half of filling mixture to within 1/2 inch (1 cm) of edges. Sprinkle with half the cherries and almonds. Beginning at the long side, roll jellyroll style. Pinch to seal seam. Cut in half lengthwise, using sharp scissors to prevent crushing. Twist halves together, keeping cut-sides up with filling visible.

5. Place on prepared baking sheet. Shape into a ring. Repeat with the remaining half of the dough. Place to make a figure "8." Pinch ends together.

6. Cover and let rise in a warm, draft-free place for 30 to 45 minutes or until doubled in volume.

7. Bake in preheated oven for 30 to 35 minutes or until kuchen sounds hollow when tapped on the bottom.

Orange Breakfast Danish

MAKES 10 DANISH		

Preheat oven to 375° F (190° C)
Baking sheet, lightly greased

1 1/4 cups	water	300 mL
2 tbsp	thawed frozen orange juice concentrate	25 mL
1/4 tsp	orange extract	1 mL
1 1/4 tsp	salt	6 mL
2 tbsp	granulated sugar	25 mL
2 tbsp	shortening	25 mL
3 1/2 cups	all-purpose flour or bread flour	875 mL
2 tsp	orange zest	10 mL
3/4 tsp	bread machine yeast	4 mL

FILLING		
1	pkg (4 oz [125 g]) cream cheese, softened	1
1/4 cup	granulated sugar	50 mL
2 tsp	thawed frozen orange juice concentrate	10 mL
1/4 cup	raspberry jam	50 mL

Easier to make than traditional Danish, these cream cheese-filled pinwheels will be a hit with your family.

TIP

Roll the ropes tightly but coil them loosely, leaving a small space between each, then flatten as you form the pinwheel. Otherwise the dough will puff up and look more like a snail than a Danish.

VARIATION

Try different jams or applesauce for the Danish centers.

1. Measure ingredients into baking pan in the order recommended by the manufacturer. Insert pan into the oven chamber. Select **Dough Cycle**.

2. Prepare filling: In a bowl, beat cream cheese together with sugar and juice concentrate until smooth.

3. Remove dough to a lightly floured board; cover with a large bowl and let rest 10 to 15 minutes. Roll out the dough into a 16- by 10-inch (40 by 25 cm) rectangle. Cut into 10 strips, 1 inch (2.5 cm) wide and 16 inches (40 cm) long.

4. On the prepared baking sheet, beginning in the center, coil each strip in a circle keeping the dough 1/4 inch (5 mm) apart. Tuck end under. Cover and let rise in a warm, draft-free place for 30 to 45 minutes or until doubled in volume.

5. Spread tops with 2 tbsp (25 mL) filling and in the center with 2 tsp (10 mL) jam. Bake in preheated oven for 15 to 20 minutes or until Danish sound hollow when tapped on the bottom.

HOLIDAY CELEBRATIONS

Ours is a multicultural nation. Our traditions live on through the passage of knowledge, food and customs from one generation to the next. We have adapted special holiday recipes for use in the bread machine. Serve these to your guests with pride.

HINTS FOR PERFECT HOLIDAY BREADS

1. Follow carefully the measurements for size and thickness as given in the recipes. The rising and baking times are based on them.

2. Measure with a steel or a plastic (not a wooden) ruler. Sanitize it in the dishwasher.

3. Make cuts with sharp scissors; a knife will often crush the filling and flatten the shape.

4. To ensure even browning when baking two pans of dough at the same time, switch their oven position at half time.

5. Sweet dough recipes brown quickly during baking because of the high sugar and fat content. If getting too dark on the top, tent with foil.

6. Use a long flat metal spatula to loosen baked shapes from the baking sheet. Slide, rather than lift, the bread onto a cooling rack.

CHRISTMAS SHAPES FOR SWEET DOUGH

Prepare a sweet dough recipe such as the LADDER LOAF (see page 138). Form using instructions given below to create a variety of Christmas shapes. Proof and bake according to instructions for LADDER LOAF.

POINSETTIA

Roll out dough into a 16- by 12-inch (40 by 30 cm) rectangle. Spread with your choice of filling to within 1/2 inch (1cm) of edge. Roll up as a jellyroll, beginning with narrow end. Cut the roll into twelve 1-inch (2.5 cm) pieces. Divide the end pieces in half. Shape into 4 balls. Center on a lightly greased baking sheet. Arrange the remaining pieces, touching, cut-side down, in a circle around the balls. Pinch the ends to form petals.

CHRISTMAS TREES

Prepare as poinsettias. Cut dough into ten 1-inch (2.5 cm) pieces and one 2-inch (5 cm) piece. Arrange, cut-side down, on a lightly greased baking sheet. Center a slice near top. Snuggly arrange the slices in three more rows, adding one more slice to each row. Center the 2-inch (5 cm) slice lengthwise under the tree for the trunk.

SWEDISH TEA RING

Prepare as poinsettias but do not cut. With the seam-side down, shape into a ring on a lightly greased baking sheet. Pinch the ends together. With scissors, make cuts two-thirds of the way through the ring, 3/4 inch (2 cm) apart. Turn each section on its side.

HOLIDAY TEDDY BEARS

Makes 1 large Teddy Bear

Divide dough in half. Form one half into a large round ball for the body. Place on a large, lightly greased baking sheet; flatten slightly. Divide the remaining piece in half. Break off a 1 1/2-inch (3.5 cm) piece and shape it into a ball for the nose. Shape the remainder of that piece into a ball for the head. Attach to the body, pinching to seal.

Make 6 balls from the remaining half of dough for the paws and the ears. Use raisins for eyes and buttons. Cover, proof and bake at 350° F for 30 to 35 minutes or until Teddy Bear sounds hollow when tapped on the bottom.

Makes 2 smaller Teddy Bears

Divide dough in half. Use one half for each Teddy Bear. Follow instructions for large Teddy Bear above. Use 3/4-inch piece for nose. Repeat with other half of dough to make a second Teddy Bear. Proof and bake at 350° F (180 °C) for 20 to 25 minutes or until Teddy Bears sounds hollow when tapped on the bottom.

Challah Braid

MAKES 1 BRAID		

Preheat oven to 375° F (190° C)
Baking sheet, lightly greased

1 cup	water	250 mL
2	eggs	2
1 1/4 tsp	salt	6 mL
3 tbsp	granulated sugar	45 mL
3 tbsp	shortening	45 mL
3 2/3 cups	all-purpose flour or bread flour	900 mL
1 tsp	bread machine yeast	5 mL

GLAZE		
1	egg yolk	1
1 tbsp	water	15 mL
1 tbsp	sesame seeds (optional)	15 mL

The Jewish Sabbath meal is not complete without this egg-rich, fine-textured bread. Serve as two braids nestled in silk or satin on a silver platter.

TIP

The easiest braid is a simple three-strand type, similar to that used for a child's hair.

VARIATION

Form dough into a 30-inch (75 cm) rope and, holding one end in place, wrap the remaining rope around to form a tight coil, higher in the center. This is traditional for the Jewish New Year.

1. Measure ingredients into baking pan in the order recommended by the manufacturer. Insert pan into the oven chamber. Select **Dough Cycle**.

2. Remove dough to a lightly floured board; cover with a large bowl and let rest for 10 to 15 minutes. Divide dough into 5 portions. Roll each with the palm of your hand into long, smooth ropes 1 inch (2.5 cm) in diameter. Taper at ends leaving the middle thicker. Braid the three ropes and place on prepared baking sheet. Twist the remaining 2 ropes, pinching ends together. Center on the top of braid. Press lightly.

3. Cover and let rise in a warm, draft-free place for 30 to 45 minutes or until doubled in volume. When dough has risen, beat together egg yolk and water. Brush the braid with glaze and, if desired, sprinkle with sesame seeds.

4. Bake in preheated oven for 30 to 35 minutes or until braid sounds hollow when tapped on the bottom.

Cranberry Orange Mini Wreaths

MAKES 10 WREATHS		

Preheat oven to 350° F (180° C)
Baking sheet, lightly greased

3/4 cup	water	175 mL
1/4 cup	cranberry juice	50 mL
1/4 cup	orange marmalade	50 mL
1/4 tsp	orange extract	2 mL
1/4 cup	skim milk powder	50 mL
1 1/2 tsp	salt	7 mL
1 tbsp	granulated sugar	15 mL
2 tbsp	butter	25 mL
2 3/4 cups	all-purpose flour or bread flour	675 mL
2 tsp	orange zest	10 mL
1 1/2 tsp	bread machine yeast	7 mL
1/2 cup	dried cranberries	125 mL

CRANBERRY FILLING		

3/4 cup	chopped dried cranberries	175 mL
1/3 cup	orange marmalade	75 mL

The perfect size for little fingers to hold and nibble while waiting to open presents on Christmas morning.

TIP

Marmalade makes an easy filling. Choose a thick, high-quality three-fruit conserve for a great taste treat.

Tuck the ends of the wreaths in tightly or they will pull out during proofing. Leave a large hole in the center of the wreath or it will close in, leaving a bun shape.

VARIATION

For a decorative holiday table, form dough into one large wreath and place a cranberry-scented pillar candle in the center.

1. Measure all ingredients *except cranberries* into baking pan in the order recommended by the manufacturer. Insert pan into the oven chamber. Select **Dough Cycle**. Add cranberries at "add ingredient" signal.

2. Prepare filling: In a bowl combine filling ingredients; set aside

3. Remove dough to a lightly floured board; cover with a large bowl and let rest for 10 to 15 minutes. Roll out dough to a 15- by 10-inch (37.5 by 25 cm) rectangle.

4. Spread half filling mixture over the middle third of the dough. Fold one side over the filling. Spread with remaining filling. Fold over last side. Cut into ten 1- by 5-inch (2.5 by 12.5 cm) strips. Holding strip at each end, pull gently, and twist 3 times. Form into a wreath, pinching ends together. Place on prepared baking sheet.

5. Cover and let rise in a warm, draft-free place for 30 to 45 minutes or until doubled in volume.

6. Bake in preheated oven for 12 to 15 minutes or until wreaths sound hollow when tapped on the bottom.

Finnish Cardamom Bread

1.5 LB (750 G)		
1 cup	evaporated milk	250 mL
1	egg	1
1 1/4 tsp	salt	6 mL
2 tbsp	granulated sugar	25 mL
2 tbsp	butter	25 mL
2 1/4 cups	all-purpose flour or bread flour	550 mL
1/2 cup	rye flour	125 mL
1 tsp	ground cardamom	5 mL
1 tsp	orange zest	5 mL
1/2 tsp	lemon zest	2 mL
1 1/4 tsp	bread machine yeast	6 mL
1/2 cup	raisins	125 mL
1/4 cup	slivered almonds	50 mL

2 LB (1 KG)		L
1 1/4 cups	evaporated milk	300 mL
2	eggs	2
1 1/4 tsp	salt	6 mL
2 tbsp	granulated sugar	25 mL
2 tbsp	butter	25 mL
2 2/3 cups	all-purpose flour or bread flour	650 mL
2/3 cup	rye flour	150 mL
2 tsp	ground cardamom	10 mL
2 tsp	orange zest	10 mL
1 tsp	lemon zest	5 mL
1 1/2 tsp	bread machine yeast	7 mL
3/4 cup	raisins	175 mL
1/2 cup	slivered almonds	125 mL

Cardamom, the second most valued spice in the world, is a favorite in Scandinavian countries.

TIP

Use cardamom as you would cinnamon — with fruits and desserts.

VARIATION

Prepare using the Dough Cycle and shape into a candy cane or tea ring.

1. Measure all ingredients *except raisins and almonds* into baking pan in the order recommended by the manufacturer. Insert pan into the oven chamber.
2. Select **Sweet Cycle**.
3. Add raisins and almonds at the "add ingredient "signal.

Easter Egg Twist

MAKES 1 TWIST		

Preheat oven to 375° F (190° C)
Baking sheet, lightly greased

1 cup	water	250 mL
2	eggs	2
1 1/4 tsp	salt	6 mL
3 tbsp	granulated sugar	45 mL
3 tbsp	shortening	45 mL
3 2/3 cups	all-purpose flour or bread flour	900 mL
1 tbsp	lemon zest	15 mL
1 1/2 tsp	cardamom	7 mL
1 tsp	bread machine yeast	5 mL

TO DYE EASTER EGGS		
1 tbsp	white vinegar	15 mL
	Food coloring	
3, 5 or 7	hard-cooked eggs	3, 5 or 7

GLAZE		
1	egg white, slightly beaten	1
1 tbsp	water	15 mL

This simple braided wreath has scarlet-colored hard-cooked eggs embedded in the rich cardamom-flavored dough.

TIP

Fruit juices, or cake decorating colors or food coloring, can be used as dyes for eggs.

VARIATION

For a crust with a shiny appearance, brush the risen dough with egg yolk before baking.

1. Measure ingredients into baking pan in the order recommended by the manufacturer. Insert pan into the oven chamber. Select **Dough Cycle**.

2. To dye eggs: In a saucepan bring to a boil vinegar, food coloring and enough water to cover eggs. Remove from heat and dip eggs until desired color is reached. (Amounts will vary with time and intensity of color desired.) Place eggs on a rack and allow to dry thoroughly.

3. Remove dough to a lightly floured board; cover with a large bowl and let rest for 10 to 15 minutes. Divide dough into thirds. Roll each piece into a 24-inch (60 cm) rope. Braid all three together. Form braid into a circle. Pinch ends to seal. Place on prepared baking sheet.

4. Press eggs into the dough at evenly spaced intervals, tucking them deep under the braids so they won't be pushed out during rising.

5. Prepare glaze: In a bowl, beat together egg white and water. Brush the glaze over the braid.

6. Cover and let rise in a warm, draft-free place for 30 to 45 minutes or until doubled in volume.

7. Bake in preheated oven for 25 to 35 minutes or until twist sounds hollow when tapped on the bottom.

Dove-Shaped Colomba Bun

Similar to an Italian panettone, but with the addition of almonds, this Easter bread is from Lombardy, Italy. The dove-shape signifies the divine protection that Milanese soldiers were thought to have received during battle in 1176.

TIP

If your bread machine doesn't have an "add ingredients" signal on Dough Cycle, gently knead the fruit into the dough as soon as the cycle finishes. Don't add extra flour or over-knead the dough; otherwise it will toughen.

VARIATION

This bread makes an attractive centerpiece for your Easter celebration. The almond paste glaze adds a festive appearance.

MAKES 1 BUN		

Preheat oven to 350° F (180° C)
Large baking sheet, lightly greased

1 cup	milk	250 mL
1	egg	1
1 tsp	salt	5 mL
1/4 cup	granulated sugar	50 mL
2 tbsp	butter	25 mL
3 1/4 cups	all-purpose flour or bread flour	800 mL
3/4 tsp	crushed anise seed	3 mL
1/4 tsp	lemon zest	1 mL
2 tsp	bread machine yeast	10 mL
1/4 cup	currants	50 mL
1/4 cup	raisins	50 mL
1/4 cup	dried candied fruit	50 mL
1/4 cup	toasted slivered almonds	50 mL

GLAZE		
1	egg white, slightly beaten	1
1/4 cup	almond paste	50 mL
2 tbsp	granulated sugar	25 mL
2 tbsp	slivered almonds	25 mL

1. Measure all ingredients *except currants, raisins, fruit and almonds* into baking pan in the order recommended by the manufacturer. Insert pan into the oven chamber. Select **Dough Cycle**. Add currants, raisins, fruit and almonds at "add ingredients" signal.

2. Prepare glaze: In a bowl combine almond paste and sugar until smooth; set aside.

3. Remove dough to a lightly floured board; cover with a large bowl and let rest for 10 to 15 minutes. Divide dough in half.

4. Make wings of the dove: Roll out half the dough to a 4- by 9-inch (10 by 23 cm) oval. Place crosswise on a large prepared baking sheet.

5. Make body of the dove: Roll out remaining dough into a triangle with a 4-inch (10 cm) base for tail, and 9 inches (23 cm) in length. Place across and on top of the wings. Hold at center, twist head one half turn clockwise, press 9-inch (23 cm) base down for tail. Squeeze head to form a beak. Cut slits 1/4 inch (5 cm) deep and 1/4 inch (5 cm) apart to form tail and wing feathers.

6. Cover and let rise in a warm, draft-free place for 30 to 45 minutes or until doubled in volume. Brush entire dove with slightly beaten egg white. Spread glaze over wings and tail. Sprinkle almonds over the glaze.

7. Bake in preheated oven for 45 to 50 minutes or until bun sounds hollow when tapped on the bottom.

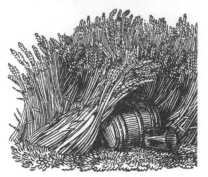

Stollen is a traditional German Christmas bread. It is served on Christmas Eve when families gather to celebrate before going to church.

TIP

With a sharp knife, make a cut 1/2 inch (1 cm) deep just off center. Fold along this line.

VARIATION

Stollen is often dusted with icing sugar to resemble a light covering of snow.

German Stollen

MAKES **2** STOLLEN		

Preheat oven to 375° F (190° C)
Baking sheet, lightly greased

1 cup	water	250 mL
2	eggs	2
1/4 cup	skim milk powder	50 mL
1 1/2 tsp	salt	7 mL
2 tbsp	granulated sugar	25 mL
2 tbsp	butter	25 mL
3 1/2 cups	all-purpose flour or bread flour	875 mL
2 tsp	lemon zest	10 mL
3/4 tsp	ground nutmeg	3 mL
1 1/4 tsp	bread machine yeast	6 mL
1/2 cup	mixed candied fruit	125 mL
1/2 cup	raisins	125 mL
1/4 cup	slivered almonds	50 mL

1. Measure all ingredients *except fruit, raisins and almonds* into baking pan in the order recommended by the manufacturer. Insert pan into oven chamber. Select **Dough Cycle**.

2. Add fruit, raisins and almonds at the "add ingredient" signal.

3. Remove dough to a lightly floured board; cover with a large bowl and let rest for 10 to 15 minutes. Divide dough in half. Roll out each half into a 9-inch (22.5 cm) circle.

4. Fold one circle almost in half with top layer set back about 1/2 inch (1 cm) from the bottom. Repeat with the other half. Place on prepared baking sheet. Cover and let rise in a warm, draft-free place for 30 to 45 minutes or until doubled in volume.

5. Bake in preheated oven for 35 to 40 minutes or until stollen sound hollow when tapped on the bottom. Dust with icing sugar while warm.

Greek Trinity Easter Bread

MAKES 1 BREAD		

Preheat oven to 375° F (190° C)
Large baking sheet, lightly greased

1 cup	water	250 mL
1/4 cup	skim milk powder	50 mL
1 tsp	salt	5 mL
2 tbsp	butter	25 mL
2 3/4 cups	all-purpose flour or bread flour	675 mL
1/2 cup	chopped dried apricots	125 mL
1/2 cup	chopped glaced cherries	125 mL
1 tsp	orange zest	5 mL
1 3/4 tsp	bread machine yeast	8 mL

Three small loaves join in a cloverleaf design for this traditional Greek Easter bread representing the Holy Trinity.

TIP

Remove from pan carefully to prevent the three sections from separating. Slice sections individually.

VARIATION

Prepare as one large circular hearth bread. Dust with icing sugar and serve warm with hot chocolate.

1. Measure ingredients into baking pan in the order recommended by the manufacturer. Insert pan into the oven chamber. Select **Dough Cycle**.
2. Remove dough to a lightly floured board; cover with a large bowl and let rest for 10 to 15 minutes. Divide dough into thirds. Form each piece into a smooth ball.
3. Arrange balls so they are just touching, in the shape of a cloverleaf, on prepared baking sheet. Cover and let rise in a warm, draft-free place for 30 to 45 minutes or until doubled in volume.
4. Bake in preheated oven for 30 to 35 minutes or until bread sounds hollow when tapped on the bottom.

Hot Cross Buns

MAKES 12 BUNS		

Preheat oven to 375° F (190° C)
Baking sheet, lightly greased

1 cup	milk	250 mL
1	egg	1
1 1/4 tsp	salt	6 mL
1/4 cup	honey	50 mL
1/4 cup	butter	50 mL
3 3/4 cups	all-purpose flour or bread flour	950 mL
1 tsp	ground cinnamon	5 mL
1/2 tsp	ground cloves	2 mL
1/4 tsp	ground nutmeg	1 mL
1 1/4 tsp	bread machine yeast	6 mL
3/4 cup	raisins	175 mL

GLAZE		
1	egg white	1
1 tbsp	water	15 mL

Before its significance for Christians, the cross symbolized the four quarters of the lunar cycle. So ancient Aztecs, Egyptians and Saxons all enjoyed hot cross buns. They have been served on Easter since the early days of the church.

TIP

Use a pastry bag and tip to pipe on icing.

VARIATION

To prepare California-style buns, add mixed candied peel and dates.

Replace milk in the icing with frozen orange juice concentrate.

1. Measure all dough ingredients *except raisins* into baking pan in the order recommended by the manufacturer. Insert pan into the oven chamber. Select **Dough Cycle**. Add raisins at the "add ingredient" signal.
2. Remove dough to a lightly floured board; cover with a large bowl and let rest for 10 to 15 minutes.
3. Divide dough into 12 portions. Roll each into a ball. Place buns at least 2 inches (5 cm) apart on prepared baking sheet and flatten slightly. Cover and let rise in a warm, draft-free place for 30 to 45 minutes or until doubled in volume.
4. Prepare glaze: In a bowl, beat together glaze ingredients; brush on dough. Make two 1/4-inch (5 mm) deep cuts in the shape of a cross on the top of each bun.
5. Bake in preheated oven for 15 to 20 minutes or until buns sound hollow when tapped on the bottom.

Italian Panettone

1.5 LB (750 G)		
3/4 cup	milk	175 mL
1	egg	1
1 tsp	salt	5 mL
2 tbsp	honey	25 mL
2 tbsp	butter	25 mL
2 1/2 cups	all-purpose flour or bread flour	625 mL
3/4 tsp	crushed anise seed	4 mL
1 1/2 tsp	bread machine yeast	7 mL
1/3 cup	currants	75 mL
1/3 cup	raisins, plumped in 2 tbsp (25 mL) brandy	75 mL
1/4 cup	candied citron	50 mL

2 LB (1 KG)		
1 cup	milk	250 mL
1	egg	1
1 tsp	salt	5 mL
2 tbsp	honey	25 mL
2 tbsp	butter	25 mL
3 1/4 cups	all-purpose flour or bread flour	800 mL
3/4 tsp	anise seed, crushed	3 mL
2 tsp	bread machine yeast	10 mL
1/2 cup	currants	125 mL
1/2 cup	raisins, plumped in 3 tbsp (40 mL) brandy	125 mL
1/3 cup	candied citron	75 mL

This festive loaf originated in Milan, Italy. It's served at Christmas and Easter, but also for weddings and christenings.

TIP

Anise gives this loaf a subtle licorice flavor. Double the amount in the recipe — or leave it out entirely to suit your family's taste.

VARIATION

Prepare this loaf using the Dough Cycle; place in a traditional high, round can, let rise and bake. The domed loaf has a soft, open texture.

Decorate the shiny crust with blanched almonds and candied cherries.

1. Measure all ingredients *except currants, raisins and citron* into baking pan in the order recommended by the manufacturer. Insert pan into the oven chamber. Select **Sweet Cycle**. Add currants, raisins and citron at the "add ingredient" signal.

Thanksgiving Harvest Twist

The sweetness of the apple contrasts with the tang of apricots and prunes in this twisted bread.

TIP

Instead of one large twist, divide all amounts in half and make two smaller ones. Keep one and give the other one as a gift.

VARIATION

Filling may be made of other readily available dried fruit such as dried apples, cranberries, blueberries or cherries.

MAKES 1 TWIST		

Preheat oven to 350° F (180° C)
Baking sheet, lightly greased

1/2 cup	milk	125 mL
1/4 cup	water	50 mL
2	egg yolks	2
1/2 tsp	salt	2 mL
2 tbsp	granulated sugar	25 mL
2 cups	all-purpose flour or bread flour	500 mL
3/4 tsp	bread machine yeast	3 mL

FRUIT FILLING		
4	Golden Delicious apples, diced	4
1 tbsp	butter	15 mL
2 tbsp	granulated sugar	25 mL
1/3 cup	coarsely chopped prunes	75 mL
1/3 cup	coarsely chopped dried apricots	75 mL

LEMON GLAZE		
2 tsp	soft butter	10 mL
1 tsp	lemon juice	5 mL
3/4 cup	sifted icing sugar	175 mL

1. Measure ingredients into baking pan in the order recommended by the manufacturer. Insert pan into the oven chamber. Select **Dough Cycle**.
2. Prepare filling: In a large frying pan cook apples, butter and sugar over medium heat, just until tender. Add prunes and apricots. Heat until warmed through. Cool before using; set aside.
3. Remove dough to a lightly floured board. Cover with a large bowl and let rest for 10 to 15 minutes. Roll the dough into a 28- by 9-inch (75 by 23 cm) rectangle.

4. Spread filling to within 1/2 inch (1 cm) of edge. Beginning at long side, roll up jellyroll style. Pinch to seal seam. Shape into large circular twist. Place on prepared baking sheet.

5. Cover and let rise in a warm, draft-free place for 30 to 45 minutes or until doubled in volume. Bake in preheated oven for 40 to 50 minutes or until twist sounds hollow when tapped on the bottom.

6. Prepare glaze: In a bowl, beat together glaze ingredients. Drizzle over warm bread.

GLOSSARY

Almonds. A popular nut with a dark tan, mottled shell enclosing an ivory-colored nut surrounded by a thin, brown skin. May be purchased whole in the shell, shelled, blanched, sliced, slivered, ground, chopped and as a paste. Two cups (500 mL) unblanched almonds weigh 12 ounces (375 g).
To blanch almonds: Allow almonds to stand, covered, in boiling water for 3 to 5 minutes; drain. Grasp the almond at one end, pressing between your thumb and index finger and the nut will pop out of the skin. Nuts are more easily chopped or slivered while still warm from blanching.
To toast almonds: Toasting intensifies the flavor. Spread nuts in a single layer on a baking sheet and toast at 350° F (180° C) for about 10 minutes, shaking the pan frequently, until lightly browned. (Or microwave, uncovered, on High for 1 to 2 minutes stirring every 30 seconds.) Nuts will darken upon cooling.

Almond extract. A concentrated flavoring made from almond oil and alcohol. Adding 1/2 tsp (2 mL) intensifies the sweet almond flavor without affecting the loaf.

Almond paste. Made of ground, blanched almonds, sugar and egg whites, almond paste is coarser, darker and less sweet than marzipan. Do not substitute one for the other.

Anise seeds/star anise. These tiny gray-green, egg-shaped seeds of the anise plant have a distinctive licorice flavor. Anise can be purchased as a finely ground powder. Use only half the amount when using powder.

Baking stone. Made of unglazed quarry or ceramic tile, the same material used to line brick ovens. Baking stones are available in different sizes and shapes. Preheat on the bottom rack of oven before using.

Brown sugar. A refined sugar with a coating of molasses can be dark, golden, or light; coarse or fine.

Bulgur. The whole wheat kernel or berry with the bran layer removed, which is then cooked, dried, and cracked into fragments. Golden brown in color, it has a nutty texture and flavor. Cracked wheat can be substituted for bulgur. Bulgur results in a coarser-textured loaf.

Butter. A spread produced from the heavy cream part of milk. Substitute using equal amounts for shortening, oil, or margarine.

Buttermilk powder. A dry powder, low in calories, that softens the texture of bread and heightens the flavor of ingredients such as chocolate. To substitute for 1 cup (250 mL) fresh buttermilk use 1 cup (250 mL) water and 1/3 cup (75 mL) buttermilk powder. It is readily available from bulk or health food stores. Keep in an airtight container as it lumps easily.

Cardamom. This popular spice is a member of the ginger family. A long, green or brown pod contains the strong, spicy, sweet-tasting, lemony-flavored seed. It is used in Middle Eastern, Indian and in Scandinavian cooking.

Caramelized onions. In a nonstick fry pan over medium heat, add 1 tbsp (15 mL) oil and 2 cups (500 mL) sliced or chopped onions and cook slowly until soft and golden. If necessary, add 1 tbsp (15 mL) water or white wine to prevent sticking.

Caraway seeds. Small, crescent-shaped, brown seeds of the caraway plant. They have a nutty, peppery licorice-like flavor.

Caper. A pickled bud of the caper bush grown in Mediterranean countries. Purchase in grocery stores in 2- to 3-oz (60 to 90 g) glass jars. Use in sauces, salads and to garnish fish and meats. Capers enhance the flavor of smoked salmon.

Cereal. Any grain that yields an edible part such as wheat, oats, rye, rice or corn. It includes the seeds or a processed product made of these seeds and grains.

Cereal, 3-Grain. *See* Red River cereal

Cereal, 7-Grain. Contains barley flakes, triticale flour, corn flakes, steel cut oats, rye meal, cracked wheat, flax seed, and hulled millet (yes, there are 8 ingredients, not 7).

Cereal, 12-Grain. Contains triticale, steel cut oats, barley flakes, sesame, buckwheat, rye meal, oats, corn, cracked wheat, millet, flax and sunflower seeds. Some others are 5-, 9- and multi-grain. All can be interchanged in bread machine recipes.

Cheddar cheese. Select a good quality aged, sharp Cheddar for bread machine recipes. The mild or medium Cheddars do not have the strength of flavor required for bread machine baking.
Weight/volume equivalents are:
4 ounces (120 g) = 1 cup (250 mL) grated;
2 ounces (60 g) = 1/2 cup (125 mL) grated;
1 1/2 ounces (45 g) = 1/3 cup (75 mL) grated.

Clay bakers. They are available in a wide variety of shapes, ranging from loaf pans to bundt pans to flower pots. Before using, grease inside completely. Although fragile, they can withstand oven temperatures.

Coffee cake. A sweet dough made with yeast which has a heavier cake-like texture.

Coriander. These tiny, yellow-ridged seeds taste of cardamom, cloves, white pepper and orange. Coriander leaves, also known as cilantro, have a flavor reminiscent of lemon, sage and caraway. To increase flavor in a bread recipe, substitute cilantro for parsley.

Cornmeal. The dried, ground kernels of white, yellow or blue corn varieties. It has a gritty texture and is available in coarse, medium and fine grind. The flavor is starchy-sweet and is used in the Southern United States as a coating or in that region's famous cornbread.

Corn syrup. A thick, sweet syrup made from cornstarch. It is available clear (light) or brown (dark). The dark variety has caramel flavor and color added.

Cracked wheat. Similar to bulgur, except that it is made from the whole grain kernel and is not pre-cooked. Either cracked wheat or bulgur can be used in bread recipes. Bulgur results in a coarser-textured, heavier loaf.

Cranberries. These small, red berries, grown in bogs on low vines, are available fresh, frozen and dried. Seasonal in nature, fresh cranberries are available only in the fall — from mid-October until Christmas, depending on your location. May be frozen right in the bag. Perfect when a tart flavor is desired. Substitute dried variety for sour cherries, raisins or currants.

Currants. Made by drying a small, seedless variety of grape, they are similar in appearance to a small, dark raisin.

Fennel seeds. Small, oval, green-brown seeds with prominent ridges and a mild anise- or licorice-like flavor and aroma. Available whole or ground, they are used in Italian and Central European cookery. The perfect seed to use in rye or pumpernickel breads.

Feta cheese. A soft, white, Greek-style cheese, with a salty, sour, tangy flavor. Store in the refrigerator in brine; drain well before crumbling.

Flax seeds. Thin, oval, dark brown seeds of the flax plant. They add a crunchy texture to breads. Research indicates that flax seeds can aid in lowering blood cholesterol levels.

Freezing dough. Seal airtight and keep up to 4 weeks. Thaw, wrapped, overnight in the refrigerator. *Refrigerating dough:* 1 to 2 hours after dough is refrigerated, dough must be punched down, then punched down every 24 hours. For the best results, use within 48 hours.

Garlic. An edible bulb (head or bud) composed of several sections (cloves), each covered with a papery layer and membrane.

To roast garlic: Cut off top to expose clove tips. Drizzle with 1/4 tsp (1 mL) olive oil, microwave on High for 70 seconds or until fork tender. (Or bake at 375° F [190° C] 15 to 20 minutes.)

To peel and mince: Use the back of a sharp knife to flatten the clove of garlic. Then the skin is can be easily removed.

Gluten. A natural protein in wheat flour that becomes elastic with the addition of moisture and kneading. Gluten traps gases produced by yeast inside the dough and causes rising. It provides strength to the dough and increases loaf volume. Gluten aids the dough in supporting added ingredients of grains, nuts and dried fruit.

Gluten flour/vital wheat gluten. When 75 to 80% gluten remains and 20 to 25% flour, it is called gluten flour or vital wheat gluten or gluten. It may be purchased from bulk food stores and added to breads with low-gluten flours for extra height.

Granulated sugar. A crystalline, white, fine grind of sucrose. It is also simply referred to as sugar or table sugar.

Hazelnut. A rich, sweet, distinctive nut that enhances coffee and chocolate flavors. It is considered to be a wild nut, while the filbert is from a cultivated tree. Remove the bitter brown skin before using. (*See* blanching almonds.)

Herbs. Annual and perennial plants whose stems, leaves or flowers are used as a flavoring, either dried or fresh. (*See also* individual herbs.) *To substitute fresh herbs for dried:* A good rule of thumb is to use three times the amount of fresh as dried. Taste and adjust the amount to suit your preference.

Honey. Used to add sweetness, honey is available as liquid, honeycomb and creamed. Use liquid honey for bread machine recipes.

Jalapeno peppers. *See* Peppers

Lame. A tool French bakers use to make perfectly shaped slashes on risen dough before baking. The blade is curved and extra sharp. This allows for the right shape of expansion as the loaf bakes.

Malt powder. Dried malt syrup. It provides a characteristic flavor, texture and crust color. It helps the loaf stay fresh longer. Store in an airtight container, as it absorbs moisture and becomes lumpy very quickly. Diastolic malt powder can be substituted using much smaller quantities than malt powder.

Margarine. A solid fat made by hydrogenating vegetable oils. Do not use low-fat margarines; they contain too much added water to produce quality loaves.

Marzipan. A sweet nut paste made from ground almonds, sugar and egg whites. Used as candy filling and cake decorations, it is sweeter and lighter in color than almond paste. (*See* almond paste.)

Mixed glazed fruit. Dried candied orange and lemon peel, citron and glazed cherries, usually dried. Frequently, expensive citron has been replaced by candied rutabaga.

Molasses. A sweet, thick, very dark brown liquid made during the refining of sugar. It has a distinctive, slightly bitter flavor and is available in fancy and blackstrap varieties. Use the fancy variety for breads. Store in the refrigerator if used infrequently.

Muesli. A cereal blend of oats, dates, sultanas, oat bran, currants, almonds, sesame seeds, walnuts, pecans, dried apples, wheat germ, flax seeds and corn grit. It should be stored in an airtight container in the refrigerator or freezer to prevent the fat from becoming rancid.

Oat bran. The outer layer of the cereal oats. It has a high content of soluble fiber, which helps to lower blood cholesterol levels.

Oat groats. Oats are steamed and rolled into flat flakes called rolled oats or old-fashioned oats. When coarsely ground oats are cooked and used for baking, it becomes oatmeal.

Oatmeal. This is a confusing term. Oats is the term used for the cereal grass of the oat grain. When the husk has been removed, it is called oat groat. *"Instant"* oats are partially cooked and dried before rolling. They are rolled thinner, cut finer, and may have flavoring ingredients added. They are not recommended for use in bread machines. *"Quick-cooking"* oats are rolled oats which are cut into smaller pieces to reduce the cooking time. For a traditional oat bread texture, use small- or medium-flake oatmeal, but not "instant cooking."
To toast oats: Spread rolled oats in a shallow pan. Bake at 350° F (180° C) 10 to 15 minutes or until brown; stir often. Store in an airtight container or freeze. Toasting oats gives a nuttier flavor.
Olive oil. Oil obtained from pressing tree-ripened olives. *Extra virgin* is taken from the first cold pressing. It is the finest and fruitiest, pale straw to pale green in color with the least amount of acid, usually less than 1%. *Virgin* contains 2% acid, a pale yellow to medium color. *Light* comes from the last pressing; it has a mild flavor, light color and up to 3% acid. It also has a higher smoke point. *Pure* has been cleaned and filtered; it is very mild-flavored and colored and has up to 3% acid.

Pastry brush. Small brush of nylon or natural bristles used to apply glazes or egg washes to the dough. Wash well after each use. To store, lay flat or hang on a hook through a hole in the handle.

Pecans. The nut of the hickory tree with a reddish, mahogany shell. The flesh is beige, has a high fat content and has two ribbed lobes. These sweeter-flavored nuts are less sharp than walnuts.

Peel. (1) The rind or skin of a fruit or vegetable.
(2) A wooden or metal, long handled blade used to move pizza or yeast breads on and off baking stones or baking sheets.

Parsley. A biennial herb with dark green, curly or flat (Italian) leaves used fresh as a flavoring or garnish. It is used as dried in soups and other mixes. Substitute parsley for half the amount of a strong-flavored herb such as basil.

Peppercorns. The berries of the pepper plant have a brown color when fully ripe. They are available in black, green, red and white. *To crack:* Use a mortar and pestle if available. Try a hammer, frypan, or a cup and bowl.

Pepper. The fruit of capsicum family with a hollow interior lined with white ribs and seeds attached at the stem end. They can be white, yellow, green, purple or red.

Peppers, bell or sweet. These have a mild, sweet flavor; seldom used as dried.

Peppers, Jalapeno. Named for the Mexican city of Jalapa, these short, tapered chili peppers have a thick flesh, are moderately hot and dark green in color.

Peppers, chili. Can be fresh or dried. *To prepare:* Wear rubber gloves to prevent burning the skin as the oil is released. Avoid touching the eyes. Most of the heat is in the seeds and ribs. *To roast:* Place whole peppers on baking sheet, piercing each near

stem with a knife. Bake at 375° F (190° C) for 18 minutes, turn and bake 15 minutes or until pepper skins blister. Place in a paper or plastic bag. Seal, set aside to cool for 10 minutes to loosen skins. Peel, discard seeds.

Pita. A hollow, Middle Eastern flatbread leavened with yeast. It is also known as pocket bread. Middle Eastern pitas tend to be oval while Greek are more round in shape.
To heat: To serve hot, heat on cookie sheet at 400° F (200° C) for about 8 minutes. For a softer sandwich, wrap in foil before heating. To microwave, place on a plate lined with paper towel and heat at High 2 to 4 minutes.
To make pita chips or crisps: Separate the layers of the pita by cutting or pulling apart. Cut both circles into 4 or 8 wedges, depending on the size of the pita. Bake, turning once, at 350° F (180° C) for 10 to 15 minutes or until lightly browned and crisp (or broil 2 to 4 minutes until golden and crisp).

Pizza wheel. A stainless steel circular wheel anchored to a handle. Use it to cut dough.

Pine nuts. The nuts of various pine trees native to China, Italy, Mexico, North Africa and southwestern United States. A shell covers the ivory colored meat, which is very rich tasting and high in fat content. Two main varieties, one mild and long shaped, the other stronger-flavored squat-triangle shaped. Substitute for any variety of nut in bread machine recipes.

Plump. To soak dried fruit in a liquid until the fruit softens and swells from absorbing the liquid. Currants are plumped in brandy, for example, in the Italian Panettone recipe.

Poppy seeds. The tiny, round, hard, blue-gray seed of the poppy has a sweet, nutty flavor. Poppy seeds are often used as a garnish.

Proof. The period of time in which shaped yeast products rise before baking.

Pumpkin seeds. Hulled and roasted pumpkin seeds, also known as *pepitas*, they are eaten as a snack and used in Mexican cuisine as a thickener. Roasting enhances the nutty flavor.

Red River cereal. It originated in the Red River Valley in Manitoba, Canada. Its nutty flavor and chewy texture comes from the 3 grains of cracked wheat, rye and flax seeds.

Rye flour. The flour milled from rye, a cereal grain or grass similar to wheat. It can be dark or light in color with low gluten content. It is always used in combination with wheat flour in bread machine recipes.

Semolina flour. A creamy yellow, coarsely ground flour milled from hard Durum wheat. It has a high gluten content. Semolina is used either alone or in combination with all-purpose or bread flour to make pasta. The semolina makes it easier to knead and hold its shape during cooking. Sprinkled on a baking sheet, it gives a crunch to Kaisers, French sticks and focaccia.

Sesame seeds. Also known as benne seeds, sesame seeds are small, flat, oval-shaped seeds with a rich, nut-like flavor when roasted. Most are available as pearly white with a glossy finish. Purchase the tan (hulled), not Black (unhulled), variety for use in a bread machine.

Shaping a loaf for loaf pan. Roll out the dough into an 11- by 8-inch (27.5 by 20 cm) rectangle. Roll up beginning at the long side, pinching to seal the seam. Place in loaf pan, seam on bottom.

Shortening. A fat made from either an animal or vegetable source; it is partially hydrogenated.

Skim milk powder. The powder that remains when fluid skim milk is dried. Use 1/4 cup (50 mL) skim milk powder for every 1 cup (250 mL) water.

Stone ground flour. The grinding of grain between two huge stones without separating the germ. It tends to be a coarser grind.

Sun-dried tomatoes. Tomatoes dried in the sun, having a dark red color, soft, chewy texture and strong tomato flavor. Sun-dried tomatoes are available either oil-packed or dried. Use dry-packed, soft sun-dried tomatoes in bread recipes. If only oil-packed are available, rinse under hot water and dry before using. Use scissors to snip each tomato half into 6 to 8 pieces.

Sunflower oil. A pale yellow, flavorless oil, high in polyunsaturated fats and low in saturated fats.

Sunflower seeds. The seeds of the familiar sunflower. With roasting comes the addition of extra salt and oil. Use raw, green, shelled, unsalted, unroasted sunflower seeds in bread machine recipes. If only the roasted, salted seeds are available, rinse under hot water and dry well before using.

Sweet potato. A tuber with a thick, dark orange skin with orange flesh that stays moist when cooked. Mistakenly called a yam, although yams can substitute for sweet potatoes in bread machine recipes.

Tarragon. A herb with narrow, pointed, dark green leaves, and a distinctive anise-like flavor with undertones of sage and a strong aroma; available fresh or dried.

Unbleached flour. Gives loaves a creamier color; may be used interchangeably with all-purpose or bread flour.

Vegetable oil. Common oils used are corn, sunflower, safflower, olive, canola, peanut and soya. They have a high polyunsaturated fat content.

Wash. A liquid applied to the surface of risen dough before baking. Frequently, milk, water, or egg are brushed on yeast dough.

Wheat berry. The berry is the whole wheat kernel which includes the endosperm, bran and germ. *To cook for use:* Cover with at least 1 inch (2.5 cm) water, and let stand overnight. Simmer for 30 to 45 minutes, stirring occasionally. Cool before using.

Wheat bran. The outer layer of the wheat berry or kernel, high in fiber and used as a cereal. Oat bran can be substituted in equal amounts.

Wheat germ. The embryo of the wheat berry which has a nutty flavor and is rich in vitamins and minerals. It is oily and must be kept in the refrigerator to prevent rancidity. Wheat germ is one of the best natural sources of Vitamin E.

White flour. A flour made by finely grinding the wheat kernel and separating out the germ and bran. It is enriched with vitamins (thiamine, niacin, riboflavin, folic acid) and minerals (iron).

Whole wheat flour. A flour made by grinding the entire wheat berry-the bran, germ and endosperm. Store in freezer to prevent rancidity.

Yeast. A tiny, single-celled living organism that requires moisture, food and the correct temperature to be active and grow.

Zahtar. This spice is an ingredient in the topping on Middle Eastern flatbread. It is available by mail order or in Middle Eastern speciality food stores. It is a blend of sesame seeds, powdered sumac and dried thyme ground together.

Zest. Strips from the colored, outermost layer of rind of citrus fruit. It is used for flavoring or frequently is candied. *To zest:* Use a zester or small sharp knife to peel off thin strips of the colored part of the skin. Be sure not to remove the bitter white part called the pith.

Zester. A tool used to cut slivers of rind from citrus. It has a short, flat blade tipped with five small holes with sharp edges.

INDEX